God's Word

Making HIM Known

God's Battle
God's Names
God's Promise
God's Providence
God's Wisdom
God's Word

God's Word

BY SALLY MICHAEL

PUBLISHING

P.O. BOX 817 • PHILLIPSBURG • NEW JERSEY 08865-0817

ISBN: 978-1-59638-859-8 (pbk)
ISBN: 978-1-59638-860-4 (ePub)
ISBN: 978-1-59638-861-1 (Mobi)

Page design and typesetting by Dawn Premako

Printed in the United States of America

Library of Congress Control Number: 2014949379

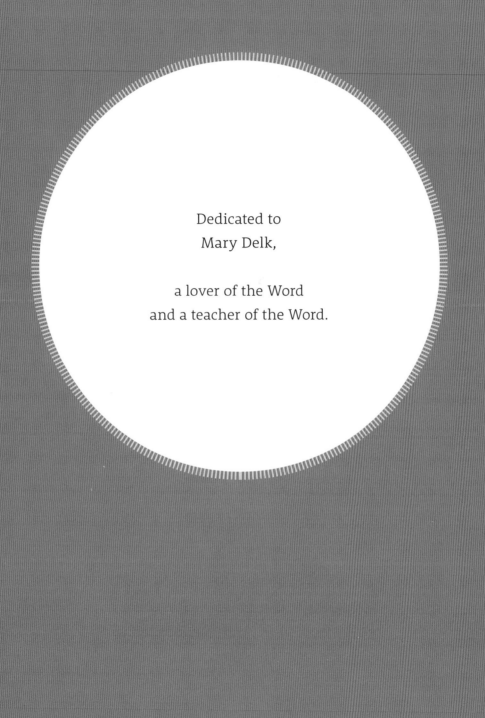

Dedicated to
Mary Delk,

a lover of the Word
and a teacher of the Word.

Open my eyes, that I may behold
wondrous things out of your law.
—Psalm 119:18

For

"All flesh is like grass
and all its glory like the flower of grass.
The grass withers, and the flower falls,
but the word of the Lord remains forever."

And this word is the good news that was preached to you.
—1 Peter 1:24–25

Contents

Preface

Forever, O LORD, your word is
firmly fixed in the heavens.
—Psalm 119:89

The Bible is God's Word for all people and for all time. It is the revelation of His character and the unveiling of His plan of salvation for sinners. It is understandable, authoritative, powerful, and unchanging.

This is the precious Word of God, which gives us hope, guidance, and protection. It was written so that we might believe—that we might believe in the one true God, eternal, unchanging, all-powerful, merciful, and just; that we might believe in His Son, Jesus, who paid the penalty for sin and opened the way to reconciliation with a Holy God; and that we might believe in the Holy Spirit, who opens blind eyes to the truth and softens hard hearts to accept God's invitation of reconciliation.

Our glorious God has given us a written record of His character, His ways, His laws, and His mighty acts so that we and our children might know Him.

He established a testimony in Jacob
    and appointed a law in Israel,
which he commanded our fathers
    to teach to their children,
that the next generation might know them,
    the children yet unborn,
and arise and tell them to their children,
    so that they should set their hope in God
and not forget the works of God,
    but keep his commandments. (Psalm 78:5–7)

God wants to be known and trusted. He wants to reconcile sinners to Himself, and He has made the truth about Himself plain in creation, through His Son, and in His Word. He has made His Word understandable . . . even to little children.

Open His Word with your child and read about our glorious God. See His mighty hand throughout the ages of history. Rejoice in His infinite faithfulness to His people and in His indescribable grace to sinful man. Stand amazed at His mighty works and His trustworthy character.

These are written so that you may believe that Jesus is the Christ, the Son of God, and that by believing you may have life in his name. (John 20:31)

The Word of God is like a lion.
You don't have to defend a lion.
All you have to do is let the lion loose,
and the lion will defend itself.

—Charles Spurgeon

Introduction
How to Use This Book

This book was written to give parents an opportunity to present solid truth to their children and to encourage real-life application of that truth.

Relational

Children receive more encouragement to learn when truth is presented by a trusted individual. Your positive, relational parent-child commitment will be a real benefit when you sit down together to read this book. Your time together over the Word should be positive, affirming, and loving.

Interactive

There is a greater impact when an individual *discovers* truth instead of just hearing it presented. Many questions have been incorporated into the text of this book to encourage your child to wonder and think critically. The process of discovery will be circumvented if you don't give your child adequate time to think and respond. After asking a question, wait for a response. If your child has difficulty, ask the question in a different way or give a few hints.

Questions and responses can be springboards for more questions and discovery as you interact with your child's mind and heart. The Holy Spirit is the real teacher, so depend on Him to give both you and your child thoughts and truths to explore together, and to bring the necessary understanding. Take the time to work through each story at a leisurely pace—giving time for interaction and further dialogue. The goal should be to get the material into the child, not just to get the child through the material.

Understandable

These stories have been written with attention given to explaining difficult or potentially new concepts. Some of these concepts may take time for your child to digest. Allow your child to ponder new truths. Read the story more than once, allowing the truth to be better understood and integrated into your child's theological framework. At times, have your child read parts of the lesson, giving an opportunity for visual learning.

Because vocabulary can be child-specific, define the particular words foreign to your child. Retell difficult sections in familiar wording, and ask questions to be sure your child understands the truth being taught.

Theological

More than just acquainting your child with an understanding of wisdom, this book is building a foundation of biblical theology for your child. As your child begins to correctly understand who God is and the wisdom of His ways, he or she won't just have a vague notion of God, but will be able to relate to the God of the Bible.

Because the Word of God has convicting and converting power, Bible texts are quoted word for word in some parts. Some of these verses may be beyond the child's understanding, so you may want to explain unfamiliar words or thoughts. Even though clear comprehension may be difficult, hearing the Word itself is a means that the Holy Spirit often uses to encourage faith in your child (Romans 10:17). Do not minimize the effectual influence of God's Word in the tender souls of children.

Since the Word of God is living and active, allow your child to read the actual Bible verses as much as possible. Also, encourage your child to memorize some of the verses so he or she can meditate on them at other times.

The gospel is presented numerous times throughout the book. Use this as an opportunity to share God's work of grace in your life, and to converse with your child about his or her spiritual condition. Be careful not to confuse spiritual interest with converting faith, and take care to avoid giving premature assurances. Fan the flames of gospel-inspired conviction and tenderness toward the sacrificial love of Jesus without prematurely encouraging your child to pray "the sinner's prayer."[1]

Application

Understanding the truth is essential, but understanding alone is insufficient. Truth must also be embraced in the heart and acted upon in daily life. Often, children cannot make the connection between a biblical truth and real-life application, so you, the parent, must help bridge the gap.

Consider the following quotation by Dr. Martyn Lloyd-Jones:

> We must always put things in the right order, and it is Truth first. . . . The heart is always to be influenced through the understanding—the mind, then the heart, then the will. . . . But God forbid that anyone should think that it ends with the intellect. It starts there, but it goes on. It then moves the heart and finally the man yields his will. He obeys, not grudgingly or unwillingly, but with the whole heart. The Christian life is a glorious perfect life that takes up and captivates the entire personality.[2]

Spend a few days or even a week on each story. Reread the story, discuss the truths, and follow the suggestions in the Learning to Trust God section. Most

---

1. Some excellent resources for parents regarding the salvation of children can be found at www.children desiringgod.org, including a booklet titled *Helping Children to Understand the Gospel* and two seminars from the 2007 Children Desiring God conference, How Great a Salvation—"Leading Children to a Solid Faith" and "Presenting the Gospel to Children."

2. D. Martyn Lloyd-Jones, *Spiritual Depression* (Grand Rapids: William B. Eerdmans, 1965), 61–62.

importantly, help your child to see that God is who He says He is, and help him or her to act in response to the truth. Point out God's involvement in daily life, thank Him for being true to His Word, and ask Him to grant you a love for His Word and a desire to follow it.

Prayer

Ultimately, our efforts are effective only if the Holy Spirit breathes on our teaching and quickens it to the heart. Pray not only before going through the stories, but also in the succeeding days, that your child would see God's character expressed in His Word, learn to live by His wisdom, and respond to Him in faith.

The Bible Is a Message from God

Have you ever played hide and seek? Where is the best hiding place in your house? When you play hide and seek, you try to hide where no one can find you. You don't want others to know where you are.

Do you think God hides, too? No, He *shows* and *tells* us who He is.[1] God wants us to know Him! All around us are messages sent to us from God to let us know who He is.

> The heavens declare the glory of God,
>> and the sky above proclaims his handiwork. (Psalm 19:1)

The world tells us about God. It shows us how great He is. It tells us that He is a great Creator.

> Day to day pours out speech,
>> and night to night reveals knowledge. (Psalm 19:2)

Every day, the world tells us about God and shows us His greatness.

> There is no speech, nor are there words,
>> whose voice is not heard. (Psalm 19:3)

God's world is a message about Himself to everyone. It doesn't matter what language a person speaks, because all kinds of people can understand what the world tells us about God.

---

1. Note that though God does reveal Himself to man, He also hides Himself from some people (e.g., those destined for destruction), and no man can ever fully comprehend the full character and nature of God (see Isaiah 45:15).

What are some ways the world tells us about God? What does God tell us about Himself through the sun and sky, birds and flowers, rivers and oceans, wind and rain?

Every day when the sun comes up, we can see that God is watching over and taking care of the world. When you see the sun in the morning, God is saying, "I'm still here. I am watching over my world." When the sun comes up in the morning and goes down at night day after day, God is sending us a message that He never changes.

At night when you see a whole sky full of stars, God is saying, "I am big. I am great." Pretty flowers are a message from God saying, "I made many beautiful things in this world. I am a good and glorious God."

All kinds of bugs—flying, creeping, and hopping . . . green, yellow, and brown . . . beautiful butterflies and strange-looking beetles— are all God's way of telling us that He is creative and never runs out of ideas. God is not boring, and He did not make a boring world!

When you see a big storm and hear loud thunder, God is saying, "I am strong and powerful." When the sun stays in the sky and doesn't fall on us, God is showing us that He rules the world with wisdom. Every day God shows us who He is. He wants us to know Him. He is not hiding.

There is another way God speaks to us, *showing* and *telling* us who He is. It is a written message. It is God's special book to us, the Bible. God wrote the Bible so we would know what He is like and what He has done.

Every story in the Bible tells us something about God. If you want to know who God is, open the Bible and read His special message to you. He will tell you what He is like, what you are like, and what He expects from you. He will tell you how you can know Him personally and what Jesus did for sinners. His word in the Bible is His message to you forever. Every page of the Bible will tell you something about the God who made the whole world and who wants you to know Him.

What has God told you about Himself in the Bible? What is He like?

All God's mighty acts and all the words He has spoken about Himself in the Bible show us what He is like. When we read about God opening the Red Sea for Israel, He is telling us that He can do anything. Nothing is too hard for Him. God is giving us the message that He takes care of His people.

What message is God giving us in the story of the flood? When we open our Bibles and read about Noah and the ark, it is not a story about animals. It is God's message to us about Himself. God is telling us that He is holy and good and that He hates sin. He sent floodwaters to destroy a world of sinners but saved Noah and his family.

When we read about Jesus healing blind Bartimaeus, God is showing us that He is kind and has power over sickness. In the story of Jesus calming the storm, God is telling us that He is stronger than anything else and is in control of all things.

The Bible is God's message to us, showing and telling us who He is. God is not hiding. He wants us to know who He is and what He is like. God wants to tell us about Himself.

I am God, and there is no other;

    I am God, and there is none like me. (Isaiah 46:9)

LEARNING TO TRUST GOD

✛ Read Acts 17:22–34. What is another way God makes Himself known to us? What does Paul say about God in these verses?

✛ Read Isaiah 46:9 again. What does this verse tell you about God?

✛ *Activity:* Explore the Bible as a family. Note that there are Old and New Testaments, and that the Bible is divided into books, chapters, and verses. Play a game to begin learning the names of the books of the Bible in order. Make cards with a book name on each card. Start with the first 5–10 cards and put them in order. Keep working on memorizing the order of the books of the Bible each week until you know them.

The Bible Was Written by God

Look at the front of this book. What is the name of the book? It is *God's Word*. What is the other name on the book? This is the name of the author, or the person who wrote the book.

Now look at a Bible. Is there an author's name on the front? Who wrote the Bible? What name would you put on the front of the Bible? Would it be Moses, who wrote the first five books of the Bible? Or Joshua, Daniel, Jeremiah, Matthew, or John? Would it be Paul, who wrote so many of the letters in the New Testament? Or would you put God's name on it?

The Bible is God's book. He wrote it so we could know Him. But we know that many men wrote the words of the Bible. So who is the real author? Maybe an example will help you to answer the question.

How would you put a screw into a piece of wood? What would you use? You would use a tool called a screwdriver. You would direct the screwdriver, putting it where it needs to be, turning it the right way, and stopping when the screw is tight. The screwdriver would not put in the screw by itself. Your hand would turn the screwdriver—it would direct and guide it.

This is similar to how the Bible was written. God was the author. But He used men to do the writing. They were like tools in God's hands. God directed them so they would write His Word. God is the real author, but He used men to write exactly what He wanted to be written.

God used more than forty different men to write the Bible, and it took them many years. Some of these men wrote more than a thousand years before Jesus was born, and others wrote after the birth of Jesus. God used all different kinds of men. He used Moses, a shepherd and leader of Israel; Joshua, an army general; David and Solomon, kings of Israel; Nehemiah, a servant; Luke, a doctor; and Paul, a teacher of religion. He used these men in different ways.

How does a small child write a letter to his grandparents? Often he tells his mother or father what he wants to say. The parent writes the words. Was it the child's letter or the parent's letter? The parent wrote the words, but the words were the child's words.

This is one of the ways God used to write the Bible. He told some of the men what to say, and they wrote the very words of God. This is what God did with Jeremiah, a prophet who tells us,

Then the LORD put out his hand and touched my mouth. And the LORD said to me,

"Behold, I have put my words in your mouth." (Jeremiah 1:9)

Over and over Jeremiah said, "The Word of the LORD came to me." God spoke to Jeremiah and told him what to say to Israel and what to write in the Bible. Jeremiah wrote the words, but the words were God's words. God was the author, and Jeremiah was His writer.

Other times, men wrote the words of the Bible with their own style and from their own experience but, even so, God guided every word of their writing. Sometimes these men wrote about things that they saw or things that Jesus told them.

> That which was from the beginning, which we have heard, which we have seen with our eyes, which we looked upon and have touched with our hands, concerning the word of life. (1 John 1:1)

John wrote about what he had seen of Jesus so we might know Jesus, that Jesus is the Son of God, and that He died on the cross for sinners. This was the message from God that He directed John to write about in the Bible.

Some of the Bible writers wrote about things they could not have known about. Daniel wrote about things that happened after he died! John wrote about the end of the world. Surely he could not know about things that have not happened yet! He hadn't seen these things. No person could tell him about the end of the world.

How could these men have written about these things that hadn't happened? They wrote about things that only God could know. God knows everything. He knows what happened a long time ago, what is happening right now, and what has not happened yet.

God showed these men what to write by giving them visions or dreams. John saw a vision of the end of the world and of heaven. Maybe it was something like a movie in John's head. Only the all-powerful and all-knowing God could show John these things.

> And he carried me away in the Spirit to a great, high mountain, and showed me the holy city Jerusalem coming down out of heaven from God, having

the glory of God, its radiance like a most rare jewel, like a jasper, clear as crystal. (Revelation 21:10–11)

John saw great troubles on earth, Jesus returning from heaven to judge and make war, and a new heaven and new earth. Then John wrote everything he had seen in the book of Revelation. The Holy Spirit gave John exactly the right words to use.

God used all these men, over all these years, in different ways just so we could have the Bible, His Word to us. He is the great Writer of the Bible, who wants us to know Him. He wants us to know that He is the Creator of the world, the Holy One of Israel, the Shield and Protector of His people, the Judge who will judge all men, and the great Savior of those who come to Him. Do you want to know this God? He has written a book so that you can. No man could write such a book. It contains the words of God, His special message to us.

For no prophecy was ever produced by the will of man, but men spoke from God as they were carried along by the Holy Spirit. (2 Peter 1:21)

LEARNING TO TRUST GOD

✛ Read Jeremiah 9:23–24. What do these verses say about what is most important? What do they say about God? Do you want to know this God?

✛ Read Revelation 22:6–9. What do these verses say about the Bible? What do they tell you to do? What do they say about God?

✛ *Activity:* Look at the Bible's table of contents. Who were some of the human writers of the Bible? Write a story together with your family, with each person independently writing a paragraph. Then read all the paragraphs. Does the story make sense? How could the Bible make sense with so many different writers living at different times writing different parts?

The Most Special Book

Books, books, books! There are *millions* of books: picture books, cookbooks, history books, math books, storybooks, textbooks . . . books about golf, books about gardening. What other kinds of books can you think of?

Out of all the books ever written, one is unique and one-of-a-kind. There is no other book like it. That book is the Bible. More than six billion copies of the Bible have been printed, and it has been translated into more languages than any other book. But this is not what makes the Bible so special.

What makes the Bible so special is that it was written by God. The God who made the whole universe and all the secrets it holds is the God who wrote the Bible. Every other book was written by a person. People make mistakes. Sometimes their information is wrong. Sometimes they can't think of the right way to say things, or they can't think of a good ending. But God doesn't have any of these problems. Because God is perfect, His book is perfect. It has no mistakes. God always knows the right way to say everything, and His story has a perfect ending.

What a wonderful book the Bible is! In it are the very words of God—the powerful, wise, and true words of the one true and living God.

> The law of the LORD is perfect,
> > reviving the soul;
> the testimony of the LORD is sure,
> > making wise the simple. (Psalm 19:7)

When we don't know what to do, God's Word can give us understanding and make us wise. When we are discouraged, His Word can make our hearts strong and new. And when we are confused, His Word shows us what is right to think and do. The precious Word of God is true, pure, and good, helping us to see what is right and giving us joy!

> The precepts of the LORD are right,
>> rejoicing the heart;
> the commandment of the LORD is pure,
>> enlightening the eyes. (Psalm 19:8)

The Bible is most special because it is the very words of the living God. The Bible is not an old, dead book that can't help us today. God's words give us life! God is living, and everything He says creates life and goodness. It goes deep

into our hearts and shows us what we are truly like. It shows us when we have sinned and when our hearts are wrong.

> For the word of God is living and active, sharper than any two-edged sword, piercing to the division of soul and of spirit, of joints and of marrow, and discerning the thoughts and intentions of the heart. (Hebrews 4:12)

The words of the Bible are precious from the very first verse to the very last verse. In this most special book written by God Himself, you can read David's words about Goliath, the giant.

> Who is this uncircumcised Philistine, that he should defy the armies of the living God? (1 Samuel 17:26)

You can find out why David could stand against Goliath and win.

> The LORD who delivered me from the paw of the lion and from the paw of the bear will deliver me from the hand of this Philistine. (1 Samuel 17:37)

You can discover what to do when you are afraid.

> When I am afraid,
>   I put my trust in you.
> In God, whose word I praise,
>   in God I trust; I shall not be afraid.
>   What can flesh do to me? (Psalm 56:3–4)

The Bible will tell you about the Red Sea splitting and the walls of Jericho falling. You will find the story of Nehemiah rebuilding the walls of Jerusalem and the story of young men escaping from a fiery furnace. You will read about Jesus walking on water, calming the storm, and healing the sick. You will learn about the crowds screaming, "Crucify Him!" and Jesus praying, "Father, forgive them." The Bible tells about Jesus coming back someday riding a white horse and wearing a robe with the name "King of kings and Lord of lords" written on it. And you can read about heaven, where there will be no tears or pain, and where God's children will see Him face to face.

What a special book the Bible is! In its pages you can find God, the Creator and King who accepts as His children everyone who comes to Him through faith in Jesus. How precious are the words of this book from God! How important are God's words for your life! Do you want to read the words of the living God in this most special book?

> More to be desired are they than gold,
>   even much fine gold;
> sweeter also than honey
>   and drippings of the honeycomb. (Psalm 19:10)

LEARNING TO TRUST GOD

+ Read Jeremiah 15:16. How did Jeremiah feel about God's words? Why? What could you say about the person who does not find God's words to be a delight? Pray for a heart that delights in God and in His Word.

+ Write Psalm 119:18 on a note card and pray it every day this week.

+ *Activity:* Have a honey snack! Discuss how the Bible is sweeter than honey and more precious than gold.

The Bible Is True

What stories do you remember hearing when you were little? Do you have memories of three pigs that built houses, a hen that baked bread, and a race between a turtle and a rabbit? These are fun stories, but are they true stories? No, they are just pretend.

God's Word, the Bible, is not like these stories. The Bible is full of true stories, even though some of them might not sound true. The Bible talks about a talking donkey, a big fish that swallowed a man and then spit him up on shore, walls that fell down when people blew trumpets, and a man who walked on water. How do you know these stories are true when they *sound* like they were made up?

We know the Bible stories are true because we know who God is. This is what Jeremiah tells us about God.

Ah, Lord God! It is you who have made the heavens and the earth by your great power and by your outstretched arm! Nothing is too hard for you. (Jeremiah 32:17)

God is God. He is not a man. He is not limited in any way. He can do all things—He created the world, made walls fall down, and told a fish to swallow a runaway prophet. Nothing is impossible for God. God can do anything, even what sounds strange and extraordinary to us. He is God.

God is not man, that he should lie,
or a son of man, that he should change his mind. (Numbers 23:19)

This God—his way is perfect;
the word of the Lord proves true. (2 Samuel 22:31)

God's words are true because God is truthful. Sometimes people lie, but God never lies. Because God never lies, everything He says is true.

Can a banana tree grow apples? Can it grow plums, grapes, or raspberries? No! Only bananas come from a banana tree. A banana tree cannot grow something that it is not. It cannot grow an apple, because it is not an apple tree. What comes from a banana tree has to be a banana.

It is the same way with God. God produces what He is. He is truthful, so what comes from God is truth. Since the Bible was written by God, and everything God says is true, then the Bible is the truth. When the Bible says Balaam's donkey talked, Balaam's donkey really talked. When the Bible says a big fish swallowed Jonah and spit him on the shore, then a big fish really swallowed Jonah and spit him on the shore. All the things the Bible says happened really happened. There are no lies in the Bible. All the miracles in the Bible really happened.

Because God is all-powerful, nothing is too hard for Him. It is easy for God to make a donkey speak. It is easy for God to make a big fish swallow Jonah and spit him on the shore. It is easy for Jesus, the Son of God, to walk on water. All these stories of miracles done by our great God are true. Nothing is too hard for God. God can do anything.

Bible stories are not pretend; they are real. We know this because God is all-powerful and truthful. The children of Israel really walked through the Red Sea on dry land, the walls of Jericho really fell down, and Jesus really did die on the cross and rise from the dead. God's book, the Bible, is a true book because God cannot lie.

The Bible also tells us about some pretend stories Jesus told. These stories are called parables. They are stories Jesus told to help us to understand things that are true. The Bible tells us these are pretend stories, saying things like, "Jesus told them a parable" or "Suppose one of you has a lost sheep." *Suppose* means "let's pretend."

This is one of Jesus' parables:

Or suppose a woman has ten silver coins and loses one. Does she not light a lamp, sweep the house and search carefully until she finds it? And when she finds it, she calls her friends and neighbors together and says, "Rejoice with me; I have found my lost coin." In the same way, I tell you, there is rejoicing in the presence of the angels of God over one lost sinner who repents. (Luke 15:8–10 NIV)

Did a lady really lose a coin? No, it is a "just suppose" kind of story that Jesus told. Jesus told us this story to help us to understand something that is true—that God and the angels in heaven are very joyful when someone turns away from sin and turns to God. The story about the lady losing her coin is not a true story. But it is true that Jesus told the story, and Jesus teaches us what is true in every story that He told.

Is the story about Jonah and the big fish a pretend story? No. The Bible does not say, "Suppose a big fish swallowed Jonah." It says that a big fish did swallow Jonah. It doesn't say that someone in the Bible was telling a parable or a pretend story about a man and a fish. It is the true story of what our great and mighty God did.

There are people who say the miracles in the Bible didn't really happen. They don't believe the Bible is true. They say God didn't make the world, the Red Sea didn't really open up, God didn't really give Moses the Ten Commandments, and Jesus didn't walk on water. How do we know these people are wrong? If these things did not happen, then God would be a liar. These people don't know who God is. They don't believe He is truthful and all-powerful.

What do you believe about God and the Bible? Do you believe God is all-powerful and truthful? Do you believe His Word is true?

LEARNING TO TRUST GOD

+ Read Daniel 3:8–4:3. How do you know that God really did rescue Shadrach, Meshach, and Abednego from the fiery furnace? What happened to Nebuchadnezzar when he saw this miracle?

+ Read Hebrews 11:1–3. What is faith? Why does it take faith to believe the Bible is true? Ask God to give you faith in who He is.

+ *Activity:* With your family, create a poster using the words, "The word of the LORD proves true." Pray and ask God to give you the faith to believe this verse.

The Bible Is for Everyone

Do you know what the words *Bleistift*, *bút chì*, *potlood*, and *lápiz* mean? They all mean the same thing. They mean "pencil" in German, Vietnamese, Dutch, and Spanish. You probably couldn't understand most of them because you speak English.

If you lived many hundreds of years ago and spoke only English, you wouldn't be able to understand the Bible either. When Moses, David, John, Paul, and others wrote the words of the Bible, they wrote in Hebrew, Aramaic, or Greek. These were the languages they spoke. Many people can't read Greek or Hebrew, so the words of the Bible were "translated" or changed into the Latin language. Changing the words of one language into words of another language is called "translating."

Six hundred years ago in England, most people couldn't understand Latin either. So they couldn't read the Latin Bible. Only priests and others with enough schooling could understand Latin. However, a young man named William Tyndale thought everyone, not just those with special learning, should be able to read the Bible. So William Tyndale decided to translate the Bible from Greek and Hebrew into English.

But there was a big problem. The king of England did not understand that the Bible is for everyone. He didn't think ordinary people should read the Bible. He thought only priests should read and explain the Bible. So it was against the law to translate the Bible into English! Even though he tried to get special permission to translate an English Bible, William Tyndale was not allowed to do so.

But translating the Bible into English wasn't just William Tyndale's idea; it was God's idea. God wants people to have the Bible in their own languages. So God gave William Tyndale the courage to leave England and go to Germany to translate the Bible. Soon parts of the Bible were translated into English. But how would these books be brought to England, where the Bible in English was forbidden?

Merchants—people who buy things in one country and bring them to another country to sell—brought the Bibles to England. Sometimes the Bibles were hidden in sacks of flour. Other times they were hidden in big rolls of wool. And sometimes they were carried into the country in traveling bags by different people. Then the books were sold to anyone who wanted to buy a Bible.

What do you think the English priests thought about this? They should have been excited that these parts of the Bible could be read by anyone. But instead they were angry! They decided to buy as many copies of William Tyndale's translation of the New Testament as they could find. What would they do with these New Testaments? Give them away? Put them in the churches? No, they burned them in a big bonfire!

But God watches over His Word, and He turns what is evil into good. With money made from selling the New Testaments that were burned, William Tyndale was able to print *many more* copies of the New Testament Bible! Now there were a lot of New Testament Bibles!

You can imagine that all these New Testaments made the king of England very angry. William Tyndale was declared a lawbreaker, and even though he knew it was dangerous, he continued his translation work until he was caught and thrown into jail. For about a year and a half, he sat in jail until he was sentenced to be strangled and burned at the stake. Just before he died, he prayed aloud, "O God! Open the King of England's eyes!"

A friend finished William Tyndale's translation, and God answered William Tyndale's prayer. Two years after William Tyndale died, King Henry the Eighth of England accepted the English Bible and ordered that the English Bible be made available in the churches to everyone in England—rich people, poor people, schooled people, unschooled people, young people, and old people.

William Tyndale was willing to die so we could have a Bible in English. He was following the plan of God, who gave him the knowledge, perseverance, and courage to translate the Bible. God made William Tyndale strong and determined not to give up, because God wants all people to read His Word. God's message in the Bible is for all people.[1]

Jesus showed this when He was on earth. When the people tried to bring the children to Jesus, the disciples scolded them—why should little children bother Jesus?

> But when Jesus saw it, he was indignant and said to them, "Let the children come to me; do not hinder them, for to such belongs the kingdom of God. Truly, I say to you, whoever does not receive the kingdom of God like a child shall not enter it." And he took them in his arms and blessed them, laying his hands on them. (Mark 10:14–16)

The disciples thought children were not important enough to see Jesus. But Jesus wants all people to hear His message. He wants all people to know Him—dishonest tax collectors like Zacchaeus, proud men like Nicodemus, wrongdoers like the thief on the cross, and little children.

1. See 1 Timothy 2:4.

Jesus wants all people everywhere to hear His words. He is not just the Savior of rich people, smart people, or Hebrew- and Greek-speaking people. He is the Savior of everyone who trusts Him. He wants His Word to be known by all peoples—including you.

> If you confess with your mouth that Jesus is Lord and believe in your heart that God raised him from the dead, you will be saved. (Romans 10:9)

LEARNING TO TRUST GOD

✦ Read Mark 10:13–16. What does this tell you about Jesus? What does Jesus mean by "receiving the kingdom of God like a child"?

✦ William Tyndale and others paid a great price so we could have the Bible in English. How much do you treasure your Bible? Do you read it daily? This week, write down one verse each day and share it with your family.

✦ *Activity:* What can your family do to support the work of Bible translation? Find a project to be involved in. Pray for missionaries you know who are translating the Bible into other languages.

The Bible Is Understandable

Have you ever been told, "You're not old enough yet"? What weren't you old enough for? Riding a two-wheeled bike? Using a knife? Staying home without a babysitter? There are some things you just can't do until you have more understanding.

But there is something you don't have to wait for. You don't have to wait to read the Bible. You can read it now because the Bible is very understandable. The most important teaching of the Bible is clear even to a child. That is why the Bible tells parents,

> And these words that I command you today shall be on your heart. You shall teach them diligently to your children, and shall talk of them when you sit in your house, and when you walk by the way, and when you lie down, and when you rise. (Deuteronomy 6:6–7)

God is not hiding! He is not covering up the truth. God wants us to know Him and the truth about sin and salvation. He has made His Word very clear so that even children can understand the most important teaching of the Bible.

Timothy was a child when his mother and grandmother taught God's Word to him. He understood their teaching and believed it. When Timothy was a young man, Paul encouraged him to keep believing the Word of God he had heard as a child.

> But as for you, continue in what you have learned and have firmly believed, knowing from whom you learned it and how from childhood you have been acquainted with the sacred writings, which are able to make you wise for salvation through faith in Christ Jesus. (2 Timothy 3:14–15)

God did not write the Bible just for adults or smart people. He wrote it so anyone can understand about creation, sin, salvation, and judgment. Who made the world? God did! The Bible makes that very clear. How did Adam and Eve sin? They sinned by rebelling against God and disobeying Him. Even children can understand this.

Why did Jesus die on the cross? Jesus died to take the punishment for man's sin. What happens when people die? They go to either heaven or hell. Those who trust in Jesus and in his payment on the cross go to heaven. Those who trust in themselves go to hell.

The Bible is not complicated. Its message is very clear. We may not understand everything in the Bible, but the most important things are easy to understand. As we grow to depend on God more and ask Him to be our teacher, we will understand the Bible even more.

There are things you understand about the sun and things you don't understand. But you understand the most important things. The sun gives us heat and light. This is not hard to understand. If you know the Bible, you also understand that God made the sun and keeps it in the sky.

You may not understand what the sun is made of or how it stays in the sky. But you do know the most important things about the sun. You are sure of them because they are very clear. If someone tells you the sun is cold, you know it's not true. You are sure it's hot and makes the world warm. What you know is clear and easy to understand. That is why you can be so certain that the sun is not cold.

The message of the Bible is clear and easy to understand, too. That is why you can be very sure of what you know. If someone tells you that God did not create the world, you can know for certain that it is not true. The Bible is clear in saying that "God created the heavens and the earth" (Genesis 1:1). That is not hard to understand.

If someone tells you that there are many ways to God, you can know for sure that it is not true. The Bible says very clearly, "There is one God, and there is one mediator between God and men, the man Christ Jesus" (1 Timothy 2:5). A mediator is someone who makes a way for you and who makes peace between you and someone else. You can know for sure that there is only one God and only one way to come to Him—through Jesus. This is very clear in the Bible.

Some people say the Bible is not clear and that you can't really understand it. But this is not true. The Bible is not hard to understand. Ordinary people can understand the main teaching of the Bible. But some people do not *want* to believe the Bible or trust God's Word. It takes faith to *believe* the Bible.[1] But any ordinary person who wants to understand the Bible, who has faith and is eager to learn from God, can see that the main message of the Bible is very clear.

You are old enough to understand the Bible, and if you ask God to help you, He will help you to understand it even more. Do you want to know what He says in His Word? Do you want to be sure of what is true? Do you want to know God? Then read His Word every day and ask Him to help you to understand it more and more.

---

1. "The natural person does not accept the things of the Spirit of God, for they are folly to him, and he is not able to understand them because they are spiritually discerned" (1 Corinthians 2:14).

Think over what I say, for the Lord will give you understanding in everything. (2 Timothy 2:7)

LEARNING TO TRUST GOD

✢ Read Deuteronomy 6:6–9. How can your family follow these instructions? Share a verse from the Bible with your family each day this week. Then explain it.

✢ Read Psalm 1. How are the two kinds of people described? What kind of person do you want to be? Ask God to teach you to love His Word.

✢ *Activity:* Do you know someone who doesn't have a Bible? With your family, buy a Bible and give it to that person with an encouraging note. (Also, don't forget to keep working on memorizing the order of the books of the Bible.)

The Bible Is about God

Baby albums sometimes tell us a baby's height and weight and when the baby was born. Sometimes they have pictures of Mom and baby, Dad and baby, brothers and sisters and baby, even Grandma and Grandpa and baby. There are pictures of all kinds of people. But who is the album about? Who is the main person in the album? The baby!

Just as there are different people in a baby album but the album is really about one person, so there are also many people in the Bible, but the Bible is about one most important person. The Bible is about God.

Adam and Eve lived and then died. Abraham lived for a time and then he died. This was true for Joseph, Moses, Joshua, King David, Esther, Jeremiah, Daniel, Matthew, and Paul. They lived for a time and then they died. They were important for a short time. But God has always been and will always be God. God is most important all the time. He is the most important person in the Bible and in the whole world.

When you read the Bible, you should notice the other people in the Bible like Abraham and David. But you should mostly be looking for God, because He is most important. What is God like? What has He done? Whenever you read the Bible or hear a Bible story or verse, ask yourself, "What does this say about God?" Every story in the Bible tells us something important about God.

What does the story of the flood tell us about God? There was such wickedness in the world that God said He would send a flood to destroy the world. He told Noah to build an ark for his family and the animals. Then God sent the flood, just like He said He would. *What does this say about God?*

It tells us that God hates sin. He is also faithful to His word—He does what He says He will do. He is a good God, protecting those who love Him. Noah and the ark is not just the story of Noah and animals. It is the story of a holy and just God who is also merciful.

After Pharaoh let the Hebrews leave Egypt, he changed his mind and sent his soldiers to bring them back. The Hebrews were caught between the Egyptians behind them and the Red Sea in front of them. Where could they go? How could they escape? God opened a path for the Hebrews through the sea, and they walked across on dry land! *What does this say about God?*

It tells us that God can do anything! He is all-powerful! He uses His power to care for His people. How strong and loving is God! He defeats soldiers and cares for His people.

Goliath was a giant of a man who hated the people of God. He challenged the Israelites to a fight, but no one wanted to fight the giant Goliath. He was such a big, strong man, and they were afraid of him! But David knew that the people of Israel were God's special people. God had helped David to fight a lion and a bear, and David knew that God would help him to fight Goliath. So David took a sling and some stones to fight against Goliath. He faced the giant . . . and threw a stone right into the giant's head, killing him! *What does this say about God?*

It tells us that God is greater than anyone—even greater than giant men. God fights for His people when they trust in Him. God made David brave and gave him skill with a sling. God gave David perfect aim and sent David's stone into the giant's head. The stone of God killed the giant Goliath! God can do anything! God is great! And He is faithful! What a wonderful God the Bible tells us about.

Haman hated the Jews and asked the king to sign an order to have them killed. But beautiful Queen Esther pleaded with the king for the lives of her people. The king listened to Queen Esther and the Jews were saved. But this story is not just about beautiful Queen Esther. It is mostly about God! *What does this say about God?*

It tells us that God knew about the Jews . . . and He knew about Haman. God had a plan to save the Jews long before He put Esther in the king's court. God is always working out His purposes. He is faithful and good. He works for His people and makes kings follow His will. God is an almighty God!

All the stories in the Bible show us how great God is. Everything He does is to show us that He can be trusted. He is not a God who hides Himself from us. He is a God who wants us to see who He is and to trust Him.

> Your way, O God, is holy.
>> What god is great like our God?
> You are the God who works wonders;
>> you have made known your might among the peoples.
>>> (Psalm 77:13–14)

When you read the Bible, remember that God is great and good. He is the most important person in the Bible—and in the world. Is He most important in your heart?

Do you want to know God? Whenever you read a story in the Bible, ask yourself, "What does this say about God?"

LEARNING TO TRUST GOD

✢ Read Exodus 17:1–7. What does this say about God?

✢ Read Daniel 4:28–37. What does this say about God?

✢ *Activity:* With your family, make a storybook for a young child using a story from the Bible. Answer the question, "What does this say about God?"

The Bible's Message: I Am God

When you get a package, are you eager to see what's inside? Is it a book, a game, clothes, or special treats? You can't wait to find out.

This is the way we should come to the Bible. What is inside? What is God's message to me today? What can I learn about God and His ways? From cover to cover on every page God tells us something about Himself.

As you read the Bible, you will discover God's unchanging message to His people. In Genesis, we read that God spoke and His words created light, the sun and the moon, the land and the sea, animals and man. God was showing us His power. Who but God can create from nothing? His message to us is, "I am God. I am not a man with weaknesses. I am the all-powerful God who needs nothing and creates all things."[1]

When God placed Adam and Eve in the garden, He told them to fill the earth and care for it. He gave them all the green plants for food, except the fruit of one tree. By doing these things, God was saying, "I am God. I am good and make all things good. I am loving, caring for your needs. I rule over all things, and my commands are sure." When Adam and Eve disobeyed and God put them out of the garden, He was saying, "I am God. I am holy and supreme. I will not allow my commands to be broken. My word stands."

God chose Abram to be the father of His chosen people, promising that they would be a great nation. God kept His promise and gave Abram a son in his old age. This is God, who is faithful to His promises. This is God, who can do anything, declaring His greatness to Abram and to us.

He told Abram, "I am God Almighty," and made a great nation from him. He brought Israel to the land He promised them, and He conquered all their enemies.

1. See Acts 17:24–25.

When Moses raised His hands to God, He gave them victory in battle. His people marched around the city of Jericho, and God caused the walls to fall down. God threw down great hailstones and stopped the sun so that Joshua could defeat the Amorites. This is God declaring, "I am God. No one can stand before me. I defeat all my enemies. I am always victorious. There is none like me."

God gave His people the ark of the covenant as a symbol of His promise to them and His presence with them. But the ark was stolen and placed in the temple of a false god named Dagon. The next morning the idol Dagon had fallen over, but the ark stood firm.

Elijah challenged the people that the false god Baal could not send fire from heaven. Though the priests of Baal cried out all day, screaming and cutting themselves with swords, Baal did not answer. Then Elijah called on God to send fire, and immediately the fire of the Lord fell from heaven. This is God Almighty declaring,

I am God, and
there is no other.
(Isaiah 46:9)

All through the Bible, God is declaring His praises.

He is showing His greatness and worth. The greatest message in the Bible is the message of who God is. He is . . .

- the Creator who made the world from nothing
- the Sovereign One who chose a people for His own
- the Rescuer who led His people out of Egypt
- the Deliverer who opened the Red Sea
- the Jealous One who judged idolatry at the feet of a golden calf with death
- the Provider who fed His people with bread and water in the wilderness
- the Victorious One who defeated all of Israel's enemies
- the King who chose David to sit on the throne of Israel
- the Judge who sent Israel to be captives in a foreign land
- the Merciful One who led His people back to the promised land to rebuild the temple and the walls of Jerusalem
- the Faithful One who fulfilled His promise to send the Messiah
- the Savior who died on a cross for the sins of men
- the Lord of Lords who will return in victory and who reigns forever!

He is the God who says,

> I am God, and there is no other;
>   I am God, and there is none like me. (Isaiah 46:9)

This is the one true God you will discover in the Bible. A God who has no equal—there is none like Him. The God who fills heaven and earth[2]—He is everywhere at all times. He never changes, His ways are perfect, and He is faithful to all His promises.

2. See Jeremiah 32:17.

God's great message to us is that HE IS GOD! Look for Him in His Word. Open the covers of the Bible and discover the great God of the universe, who needs nothing and yet who left heaven to come as a man to die for sin so that we could become His children.

LEARNING TO TRUST GOD

+ Read Psalm 8:3–4. What difference does the psalmist show between God and man? What is his attitude?

+ Read Romans 11:33–36. What does this tell you about God? How is He different from man?

+ *Activity:* Read Psalm 96 with your family. Then make up a song, poem, cheer, or rap declaring the greatness of God. Thank Him for being God, and ask Him to open your eyes to see His greatness.

The Bible's Message: There Is No Other God

Can a cat decide to become a lion? Can he say, "I'm tired of being a cat. I want to be the king of beasts," and become a lion? Could a cat ever go up to a lion and say, "I'll fight you for the right to be the king of the beasts"? What would happen? Would the cat ever win?

Well, something like this happened. God created all the angels to serve and worship Him, but there was one angel who wanted God's throne. He was not God; he was an angel. He was less than God. He was not as powerful, wise, good, loving, or in any way as great as God is—just like a cat is not a lion. But Satan decided that he wanted to be like God, so he and some other angels fought against God.[1]

But can a cat win against a lion? No! Neither could weak Satan win against the strong God of the universe. God threw Satan, and the angels that followed him, out of heaven. We know Lucifer as the Devil or Satan. He is the enemy of God. He hates God and wants everyone else to hate God too.

Satan could not take God's place. Only God is God, and He will not give His place to anyone else. This is what God says in the Bible:

> You shall have no other gods before me.
>
> You shall not make for yourself a carved image, or any likeness of anything. . . . You shall not bow down to them or serve them, for I the Lord your God am a jealous God. (Exodus 20:3–5)

What do these verses tell us? If someone takes a knife and carves an idol, would this pretend god be greater than God? If this person put gold and precious

---

1. See Isaiah 14:12–14; 2 Peter 2:4; Jude 6.

jewels on the idol, then would it be greater than God? Could it do powerful things, know all things, or help the person when he has a problem?

No, it can't. But this is what people sometimes do.

A tree from the forest is cut down
    and worked with an axe by the hands of a craftsman.
They decorate it with silver and gold;
    they fasten it with hammer and nails
    so that it cannot move.
Their idols are like scarecrows in a cucumber field,
    and they cannot speak;

I, You shall have no other gods before me.

they have to be carried,
    for they cannot walk.
Do not be afraid of them,
    for they cannot do evil,
    neither is it in them to do good.

There is none like you, O LORD;
    you are great, and your name is great in might. (Jeremiah 10:3–6)

An idol could never take the place of God. It can't speak or walk or do anything. But our God acts! He sends lightning and rain, parts the sea, makes the sun come up every morning, sends manna bread from heaven, and wins battles for His people. God is the only true God.

It seems silly to us to bow down to idols and tell them that they are great. Something made of wood, stone, or even gold cannot be powerful, answer prayer, or make things happen in the world.

We may not bow down to wooden or stone idols, but we can put other things in God's place. When we make anything most important in our hearts, we are putting it in God's place. He is most important. Only God should be in first place. Only God is the greatest and the best.

What things could a person love more than they love God? What things can become more important in our hearts than God is?

Some people love money. They are always thinking about how they can get more money. When they have a problem, instead of praying, they turn to their money to help them. They feel very protected when they have a lot of money, thinking, "Money will buy me another car when my car breaks, and money can make me happy with a fun vacation."

But can money make them better if they have a sickness that no medicine can cure? Money is not all-powerful. Only God is all-powerful. Money cannot do all things. Only God can do all things. Only God is worthy to be in first place in our hearts.

Other people love to feel important. They want everyone to think they are wonderful. Can they ever be as wonderful as God? No! They make mistakes and they sin. Sometimes they treat others unkindly, and they think mostly of themselves. They are putting another god in God's place. Their god is themselves. They love themselves most of all.

Some people love having fun more than anything else. They are always looking for more and more fun things. But then they get bored. They cannot find the joy that comes only when we make God most important in our hearts.

Then there are people who make another person the most important person in their lives. Do other people love perfectly? No. Sometimes people hurt us. They can be selfish or unkind. They can never be as faithful and loving as God is.

Only God is God. Only God is the greatest and is worthy of our deepest love and respect. He will not let anyone or anything take His place.

What is most important in your heart?

You shall have no other gods before me. (Exodus 20:3)

LEARNING TO TRUST GOD

✛ Read 1 Samuel 5:1–4. What does this tell you about God?

✛ How can you tell what is most important in your heart? Read Psalm 42:1. What does this tell you about the place that God should have in our hearts?

✛ *Activity:* There are people who have never heard of the one true God. How can they worship Him if they have not heard of Him? With your family, pray for a missionary family working among unreached people. What can your family do to encourage them?

The Bible's Message: Created to Show God's Greatness

Have you ever made something by yourself? What was it? When you make something, the thing you make shows other people something about who you are. A nicely colored picture shows someone that you are careful. But a picture with scribbling outside the coloring lines might show that you are sloppy or don't like to color.

A delicious meal might show you that the person who made it is a good cook. But a handmade chair that is crooked and wobbly would show you that the builder has a lot to learn about making chairs!

Everything in the world tells us about the Maker of the world. What does lightning show us about God? It shows us that God is very powerful!

What do buzzing flies, creeping beetles, wiggly worms, and jumping grasshoppers tell us about God? They tell us that God has a good imagination. He is very creative and does not run out of ideas.

The vast universe with all the stars and planets that stretch across the sky shows us that God is big. He is greater than all things. By His hand, He created the world and everything in it. All creation was made to tell us about the greatness and worth of God.

The heavens declare the glory of God,
and the sky above proclaims his handiwork. (Psalm 19:1)

Creation shows us God's glory—it shows us that He is a great God. Every time we look at the world God has made, we should remind ourselves of what it tells us about God. Then we should be amazed at who He is and should praise Him like this:

Bless the LORD, O my soul!
    O LORD my God, you are very great!
You are clothed with splendor and majesty,

. . . .
You make springs gush forth in the valleys;
    they flow between the hills;

. . . .
You cause the grass to grow for the livestock
    and plants for man to cultivate,

that he may bring forth food from the earth

. . . .

You make darkness, and it is night,
    when all the beasts of the forest creep about.

. . . .

O Lᴏʀᴅ, how manifold are your works!
    In wisdom have you made them all;
    the earth is full of your creatures.
Here is the sea, great and wide,
    which teems with creatures innumerable,
    living things both small and great.

. . . .

May the glory of the Lᴏʀᴅ endure forever.
    (Psalm 104:1, 10, 14, 20, 24–25, 31)

Everything God made, He made to show how great He is. God made people for the same reason—to show His *glory*[1], His greatness, and His worth. All day and every day we breathe in and out without even thinking about it. What does this show the world about God? He keeps life going. His invisible hand takes care of us and His world. Isn't He a great and good God?

Cuts that heal and broken bones that grow back together show that God is an amazing God! The things that we make can't do this. When we tear a piece of clothing, it doesn't grow back together.

When we do something kind for someone, we are showing the world God's nature. We are showing the world what God is like—that He is kind and good.

When a mom hugs a child, it is a reminder that God is loving and kind. When a man picks up something heavy, it is a reminder that God is strong. God created people, just like the rest of His creation, to show off God's greatness.

1. See Isaiah 43:1–7.

But instead of showing God's greatness and worth, people often want themselves to look great. This is what happened in Babel when the people said,

> Come, let us build ourselves a city and a tower with its top in the heavens, and let us make a name for ourselves, lest we be dispersed over the face of the whole earth. (Genesis 11:4)

They did not care about showing God's greatness. They wanted to show their own greatness, to "make a name for themselves." How high could their tower be? How could it compare to putting the moon in the sky, or making a tall oak tree from a small acorn? Thinking that they were so great showed that they did not understand the greatness of God. How foolish to brag about themselves when God is so much greater!

Do you know what God did to the people at Babel? He made them speak different languages so they could not build their big tower. They could no longer understand each other or work together. God made a name for Himself when He stopped their tower-building. He showed His greatness and worth to weak, foolish men.

The great God of the universe did not create people so that our smallness could be seen, but so that we would praise God for His greatness. Do you want to show God's greatness and worth? How can you show others how great He is?

LEARNING TO TRUST GOD

✦ Read Psalm 104:1–15. What do these verses show you about God's greatness and worth?

✦ Read Psalm 104:16–35. How does creation show the greatness of God? This week, tell someone about the greatness of God.

✦ *Activity:* Start a nature collection to show the greatness of God (e.g., bugs, flowers, shells, rocks, leaves). When your collection grows, share it with someone else, and explain that everything in the world was created to show God's glory.

The Bible's Message: All Have Sinned

Suppose you want to eat an apple. There are two apples in your refrigerator. One is soft and mushy with brown spots, and the other is firm and crisp. Which one would you choose? It would be foolish to choose the rotten apple, wouldn't it? By choosing the crisp apple you are showing that it is the best one—it has the greatest worth or good.

But we don't always choose the best. Sometimes we choose very foolishly. The Bible tells us about the most foolish choice in the whole world. Can you guess what it was?

God placed Adam and Even in the garden of Eden. It must have been a very beautiful garden without weeds and full of luscious fruits to eat. God said Adam and Eve could eat from any of the trees in the garden except the one in the middle of the garden. Do you think God had the right to make this rule? Yes, He did because He is the Creator and Owner of all things. He is also wisest, and He knew what was good for Adam and Eve.

But Satan came in the form of a serpent or snake and lied to Eve.

But the serpent said to the woman, "You will not surely die. For God knows that when you eat of it your eyes will be opened, and you will be like God, knowing good and evil." So when the woman saw that the tree was good for food, and that it was a delight to the eyes, and that the tree was to be desired to make one wise, she took of its fruit and ate, and she also gave some to her husband who was with her, and he ate. (Genesis 3:4–6)

Do you remember why Eve and all things were created? They were all created to show God's glory—to show God's greatness and worth. But Eve didn't want to show God's greatness. She wanted to be great herself! She wanted to be like God.

Does this sound familiar? This is just what Lucifer wanted. He wanted to be like God. But of course he could not fight against God and win. Now he was trying to get Eve to do the same thing.

What would Eve do? Would she be happy to show the greatness and worth of God, and worship Him as the Most High? No, instead Eve chose to disobey God. She didn't choose the greatest joy of worshipping God. Instead, she chose

to sin. This is like choosing the mushy, rotten fruit instead of the good fruit . . . only millions of times worse!

Adam made the same choice. Just like Eve, he disobeyed God. He wanted his own glory more than he wanted God. So he ate the fruit too.

When Adam and Eve heard God walking in the garden, they hid themselves. They knew they had done wrong, and they were afraid. But God cannot be fooled. He knew about their sin, and He knew they had to be punished. Adam and Eve had to leave the beautiful garden where they met with God, and they could never return.

Because of Adam's sin, sin came into the world. Adam and Eve had children, and their children had children, and those children had children. Everyone who has come from them is a sinner, just like their parents.[1]

When a hen (a female chicken) lays an egg, what hatches from the egg? Will turtles hatch from hen eggs? How about lizards or snakes? Baby chickens called chicks come from hens. What is born to the parents will be like the parents.

Just as chicks come from hens, lizards come from lizards, and snakes come from snakes, so sinners come from sinners.[2] So everyone who has ever lived or ever will live, except Jesus, is a sinner. Everyone by nature lives for his own glory and not for God's glory.

For all have sinned and fall short of the glory of God. (Romans 3:23)

Did anyone have to teach you to disobey? No, it was just in you when you were born. You were born with a desire to sin. The problem is not just that "we do bad things," but that we are born with hearts that do not want to love God or what is right. We do not love the goodness and worth of God, so we do not bring

1. This does not include Jesus, who was born from Mary but not from a human father. The sin of humanity was not transmitted to Him.
2. See Romans 5:12.

glory to God. Our sinful hearts do not want to give God first place. Not only do we sin, but we are sinners. Sinners love other things more than they love God.

> None is righteous, no, not one;
>> no one understands;
>> no one seeks for God. (Romans 3:10–11)

This is God's message about us in the Bible. Our hearts do not naturally turn toward God. They turn away from Him. But the Bible also has another message for us—a wonderful message for sinners. It gives us hope that we can live to show God's greatness and worth, just like we were made to do.

LEARNING TO TRUST GOD

✛ Read Genesis 3:1–13. What happened to Adam and Eve's relationship with God when they sinned? What do these verses tell you about God?

✛ Read Genesis 4:1–7. What does verse 7 mean?

✛ *Activity:* Because of our sinful hearts, "no one seeks for God" (Romans 3:11). But God does seek for sinners. Read Luke 19:10. Then make a list of people who you know are not seeking God and pray for them as a family.

The Bible's Message: The Wages of Sin

What is your favorite thing to drink? Is it a cool glass of milk . . . with a chocolate chip cookie? Is it icy lemonade on a hot day? Maybe your favorite drink is steaming hot chocolate on a freezing winter day.

If your favorite drink had just a small spoonful of dirt in it, would you want to drink it? Why not? Most of the drink is okay. Most of the dirt would probably sink to the bottom. Couldn't you just drink some of it? No, you would throw the drink away. It is no good, even with just a little dirt.

Do you know that, in a way, we are like that drink? The milk, lemonade, or hot chocolate is like our hearts or souls—the part of us that desires good or evil. The dirt is our sin nature—not just the sins we have done, but our desire for sin. That makes our whole heart or soul dirty. It is not pure and good and right before God.

So what should God do with us? Should He throw us away like a drink with dirt in it? After all, the Bible says,

> None is righteous, no, not one;
>> no one understands;
>> no one seeks for God. (Romans 3:10–11)

No one is righteous. No one is without sin. All of us have a sin nature, and our sin nature makes us unacceptable to God. We are unacceptable—like a drink with dirt in it.

Would a person who wants to be healthy drink something with dirt in it? No, he would want something clean. God is the same way. There is no sin in God; He is sinless. He is pure and good and right and full of love. Just like a healthy person would not accept a dirty drink, so God cannot accept a sinful heart. God hates sin.

What happened when Adam and Eve sinned? They were punished for their sin. God is perfect and without sin, so He must punish sin. He cannot ignore it or pretend it is not there. Just like Adam and Eve were punished, we too must be punished for sin.

What is something you were punished for? Did you get to decide the punishment by yourself? Who decided the punishment? Your mother or father, or

the person in charge decides the punishment. That person makes the rules and decides the punishment. Could you change the punishment? Why not? You can't change the punishment because you are not in charge.

God is in charge of the whole world, and He decides the punishment for sin. Can we change the punishment? No, we are not in charge. Can we decide that we should not be punished? No, we do not rule the world. God does. He is in charge, and only God can decide about the punishment.

Do you know the punishment for sin?

For the wages of sin is death. (Romans 6:23)

"The wages of sin" is another way of saying "the punishment for sin." God has decided that the punishment for sin is death—not just death to our bodies, but also death to our souls. Just as Adam's and Eve's sin meant they could not live in the garden of Eden with God, so our sin means we cannot live in heaven with God. Instead, the punishment for sin is hell. Hell is a place of sadness and pain where we will be apart from God and all His goodness forever.

This is how awful sin is. Even one sin keeps us from heaven and from being with God. So what can we do about the many times we sin, and what can we do about our sinful hearts?

We can't do anything. It is too late. We cannot change the punishment, and we cannot change our hearts.

But this is not the end of God's message. Look at the verse below about the wages of sin. What do you see at the end of the last word? Do you see three dots like this: . . . ? This is called an ellipsis. It means something was left out. This is not the whole verse. The end of the verse was left out in our story. And the end of the verse has good news for sinners! If you look up the verse in the Bible, you will get a sneak preview of the next story.

For the wages of sin is death . . . (Romans 6:23)

God's message in the Bible about sinful hearts is very bad news, but He has more to tell us in His Word. He has good news too.

LEARNING TO TRUST GOD

✢ Read Genesis 3:14–24. What punishment came from Adam's and Eve's sin? Where do you see God's goodness in these verses?

✢ Read Matthew 13:47–50. Explain this story that Jesus told. What is hell like? What hope does the story give us?

✢ *Activity:* Visit a cemetery and read some of the tombstones. Remind yourself that everyone dies, and his or her physical life is over. But the soul continues in either heaven or hell. Ask God to show you the seriousness of your sin. Thank Him that there is also good news.

The Bible's Message: Saved by Grace

Have you ever fixed something? If so, what did you fix?

Some things can be fixed. A tear in your shirt can be sewn together. A flat tire can be fixed with a patch. But some things can't be fixed. A squirrel that has been run over by a car can't be fixed. Neither can a rotten tomato.

We all have something we cannot fix. We cannot fix our sin problem. Every one of us was born with a sin nature. We were born with hearts that want to sin. We cannot fix that, just like we cannot fix a rotten tomato.

Some people think they can fix the sin problem by doing good things. But they are wrong. Could you fix a glass of milk with dirt in it just by adding sugar? No, the dirt is still in the glass. The sugar doesn't take out the dirt. Neither does doing good things along with the bad things we do take away our sin nature. Our sin nature leads us to more and more sin. Sinful hearts can't be fixed by us. It takes an all-powerful, all-loving, all-knowing God to fix a sinful heart.

Do you know how God fixes sinful hearts? He actually gives a person a *new* heart! Our hearts are like stone. They are hard—we do not love God. We are always thinking of ourselves and what we want. We hurt other people. We do not want to read the Bible or pray. And we love sin and want to get our own way. What does God do with that heart of stone?

And I will give you a new heart, and a new spirit I will put within you. And I will remove the heart of stone from your flesh and give you a heart of flesh. (Ezekiel 36:26)

New hearts of flesh want to trust God and do what is good and right. New hearts of flesh hate sin and love God's ways. How wonderful of God to change hearts of stone to new hearts of flesh!

But what about the punishment? God said that the punishment for sin is death—being in hell forever and separated from God. We can't change the punishment for sin, even with a new heart. But God did the most unimaginable thing in the whole world! He sent His Son, Jesus, to take the punishment!

He himself bore our sins in his body on the tree, that we might die to sin and live to righteousness. By his wounds you have been healed. (1 Peter 2:24)

The punishment for our sin is death—either our own eternal death in hell, or Jesus' death on the cross. Jesus took the punishment that belongs to sinful man! When God gives a person a new heart of flesh, that person is able to trust Jesus as His Savior. He trusts Jesus' payment for sin on the cross. But not only does Jesus take the punishment for sin, He also gives those who trust in Him a gift!

Do you remember about the ellipsis? Here is the whole verse without the ellipsis. The rest of the verse tells us about the free gift.

> For the wages of sin is death, but the free gift of God is eternal life in Christ Jesus our Lord. (Romans 6:23)

The first part of the verse is horrible news. But the last part of the verse is the greatest news of all! Instead of hell, those who are trusting in Jesus get heaven! Now that is a magnificent gift! Can you even imagine a better gift than this? There is no greater gift.

Why would God give sinful men such an incredible gift? It isn't because we deserve it. He gives it because He is good and kind. Isn't that absolutely amazing?

It is amazing. But some people don't want God's gift of salvation, and some people think they don't need God's gift. They think they can be good enough and do enough good things to go to heaven without Jesus' payment. But these people are wrong. They are turning away the greatest gift in the world.

What will you do with God's gift? What is in your heart? Can your heart attitude be described like this heart of flesh?

> "I trust you, God. I believe everything in your Bible. You are so good to me. I need to be forgiven for my sins. I cannot take care of my sin problem. I do not want to have this sin in my life. Only you can save me from my sins. I do not deserve your gift. Thank you for being a good God."

A heart of flesh is a gift from God. Have you asked God for a heart of flesh?

> For by grace you have been saved through faith. And this is not your own doing; it is the gift of God, not a result of works, so that no one may boast. (Ephesians 2:8–9)

LEARNING TO TRUST GOD

+ Read Ephesians 2:8–9 again. Then explain it to your mother or father. What does this tell you about God?

+ Read Ezekiel 36:22–29. Ask your mother or father to help you to understand these verses. Was Israel living to show God's greatness and worth? What does God mean when He talks about "for the sake of my holy name"? What is the difference between a heart of stone and a heart of flesh? Do you want to pray that God would give you a heart of flesh?

+ *Activity:* God's gift of grace is undeserved. What is it like to receive a gift you don't deserve? Think of someone your family can give a gift to for no reason at all—not a birthday or Christmas gift, but just a gift to demonstrate the good and kind heart of God. Pray for that person and deliver the gift.

The Bible's Message: God's Gift of Eternal Life

C an you think of something that is both good and bad? For example, candy is both good and bad. It tastes good, and we like it. But it is not the healthiest food. Rain is both good and bad. It is good because we need water to drink and to water the fields. But if you want to go on a picnic, rain isn't so good, and too much rain can cause flooding. Can you think of anything else that is both bad and good?

Life on earth is both bad and good too. The earth is full of beautiful trees and puffy clouds, rushing rivers and majestic mountains, interesting animals and colorful, sweet–smelling flowers, warm sunshine and icy snowflakes. There are also good friends and loving families. There are so many good things God gave us here on earth.

But there are bad things here too, like sickness, pain, lying, stealing, and all kinds of sin. All of these are part of the evil that came into the world through Adam's and Eve's sin.

Stephen was a follower of Jesus who knew about the good and the bad . . . and the very best. The Bible says that Stephen was "full of faith" (Acts 6:5). He spoke to the Jews about God's faithfulness to them and their hard hearts. This made the Jews so angry that they "ground their teeth at him."

But he, full of the Holy Spirit, gazed into heaven and saw the glory of God, and Jesus standing at the right hand of God. (Acts 7:55)

It was the moment of Stephen's death. But God allowed Stephen to see what waited for him after he died. How good of God to let Stephen see the best. Stephen would leave the good and the bad to get the very best in heaven forever. He would be with God the Father and Jesus the Son.

The Jews dragged Stephen out of the city and stoned him to death. That was just physical death for Stephen. His body would die, but his soul would live on with God.

Heaven is the most wonderful place, because it is the home of God. All those who are trusting in Jesus are promised a place in heaven. When Jesus told the disciples that he would be going away before He went to die on the cross, He also told them this:

In my Father's house are many rooms. If it were not so, would I have told you that I go to prepare a place for you? And if I go and prepare a place for you, I will come again and will take you to myself, that where I am you may be also. (John 14:2–3)

Jesus is waiting for those who trust in Him to come to heaven to live with Him. He is getting heaven ready for us!

He is excited about sharing heaven with us. Heaven is a beautiful place. It is not just a big house—it is a whole other world. It is a world where there is no sickness or death. There will be no crying or pain in heaven. Heaven is a place of joy and peace. Heaven is the very best place, because God lives in heaven.

Have you ever wondered what heaven is like? We can't even really imagine it because we have never seen such a beautiful place. We live in a sinful world, so we can't imagine a world with no sin, sadness, or suffering. We can't imagine what it will be like to live forever in joy with Jesus.

Sometimes we are afraid or nervous about things we don't know much about. Will heaven be like going to a new church where you don't know anyone, or meeting a new teacher in a new class? Those things can make us a little nervous. But if Jesus is your Savior, going to heaven will be very different from what it is like now to go somewhere unfamiliar. Jesus will be in heaven. We will finally be going to see our very best friend face-to-face. He will always care for us there, and nothing bad will be there. If you are a child of God, you have the best place waiting for you. Jesus is there making heaven the perfect home for His children.

Do you want to go there someday? You will, if you are trusting Jesus as your Savior and living to show God's greatness and worth, and if God has given you a heart of flesh so that you love Him and all that He loves. Jesus will come again to bring all His children home with Him. What a wonderful day that will be!

And I heard a loud voice from the throne saying, "Behold, the dwelling place of God is with man. He will dwell with them, and they will be his people, and God himself will be with them as their God. He will wipe away every tear from their eyes, and death shall be no more, neither shall there be mourning, nor crying, nor pain anymore, for the former things have passed away." (Revelation 21:3–4)

LEARNING TO TRUST GOD

✦ Read John 14:1–6. What does Jesus mean by "believe in me"? What does Jesus mean when He says that He is "the way, the truth, and the life"? Ask God to give you true faith in Jesus.

✦ Read Revelation 21. How is heaven described?

✦ *Activity:* Go to a jewelry store and find some of the jewels described in Revelation 21:18–21. How would you describe these jewels? Why would they be used to describe heaven?

God Keeps His Word

How do we know God will actually keep His Word? Maybe something will happen, and He won't be able to do what He said He will do. Maybe He will forget. Or maybe He will change His mind.

None of these things will happen. Nothing will happen to stop God, who is all-powerful. He never forgets what He says, and He doesn't change. Maybe understanding how pudding is made will show you that you can trust that God will always keep His Word.

Pudding? Did you say pudding? What does pudding have to do with God?

Well, have you ever made pudding—not the instant kind, but the kind you have to cook on the stove? The instructions say to put all the ingredients in a pan and then heat the pudding on the stove, *stirring constantly*. Stirring constantly is very important. If you walk away, the pudding might boil over and make a mess. Or it could burn on the bottom of the pan, which will spoil the taste. Burnt pudding just doesn't taste good!

But if you are stirring constantly, you are watching over your pudding. If it gets too hot or starts to bubble too much, you keep stirring and turn down the heat. Because you are carefully watching over your pudding, you keep it from burning or bubbling over.

This is like the way God acts in the world. He is living and active. He is not sleeping. He is "stirring constantly." He doesn't walk away from the world and just hope things work out. He watches over every little thing in the universe. *Nothing* is ever outside His control.

This is how we know that God keeps His Word. He is always watching to make sure His Word comes true. He doesn't just hope it works out. He makes it work out.

For I am watching over my word to perform it. (Jeremiah 1:12)

What God says He will do, He does. Because God has everything, He never runs out of anything. He is also strong. In fact, He is all-powerful, so there is nothing He cannot do. He knows everything, so nothing is a surprise to Him. He is constantly watching over His Word. So He is always able and willing to keep His Word.

We already know that everything the Bible said happened, really happened. Every verse in the Bible is true. And everything God says He will do, He *will* do.

Almost 750 years before Jesus was born, it was written in the Old Testament that Jesus would be born in a city called Bethlehem.

> But you, O Bethlehem Ephrathah,
>> who are too little to be among the clans of Judah,
> from you shall come forth for me
>> one who is to be ruler in Israel,
> whose coming forth is from of old,
>> from ancient days. (Micah 5:2)

Did God keep His promise? Did He do what He said He would do? Almost 750 years after Micah wrote about God's promise to send Jesus, Matthew wrote what actually happened.

> Now after Jesus was born in Bethlehem of Judea in the days of Herod the king, behold, wise men from the east came to Jerusalem. (Matthew 2:1)

It happened just like God said it would! How did this happen? Did God say that Jesus would be born in Bethlehem, and then worry about whether it would happen that way? Did He go to sleep for 750 years and wake up to see if it really happened? No! When God says something will happen, He makes it happen! He watches over His Word, and He makes sure it is done as He has said. God has all power, all knowledge, and everything He needs to make sure that what He says will happen does happen.

> For I am watching over my word to perform it. (Jeremiah 1:12)

How could Jesus be born in Bethlehem when Mary and Joseph lived in Nazareth? This sounds like a big problem. But it wasn't a problem for God. He is always watching over His Word, and He has the power to make His Word come true. So how did God make the birth of Jesus happen in Bethlehem?

God gave Caesar Augustus, the ruler of the Roman Empire, the idea to count the people. So Caesar made a law that everyone had to return to the place their family came from to be counted. Joseph's family was from Bethlehem, so Joseph and Mary went there . . . and Jesus was born while Mary and Joseph were in Bethlehem, just as God said would happen.

Why did the king decide to count the people, and to make them go back to the place that their family came from? God put that idea in the king's mind. God was watching over His Word. *God makes His Word come true!*

> As I have planned,
>   so shall it be,
> and as I have purposed,
>   so shall it stand. (Isaiah 14:24)

LEARNING TO TRUST GOD

+ Read Joshua's words to Israel in Joshua 23:14. What does this tell you about God's faithfulness to keep His Word? How can this give you confidence in the Word of God?

+ Read Psalm 105:8. Figure out how long a thousand generations is. (You can use 40 years as the length of a generation.) What does this tell you about God's faithfulness to His Word?

+ *Activity:* Make cook-and-serve pudding. Be sure to constantly stir it. How is this like God's care over the world and His Word? Make a pie with your pudding, or serve it with whipped cream. Share it with someone, explaining to that person how pudding can help us to understand that we can trust God to keep His Word.

The Bible Is Unchanging

All kinds of things change. For example, the weather changes. It is not always sunny or always rainy. Leaves also change. They change from green in summer to red, yellow, and brown in the fall. Even hair changes. When people get older, their hair turns gray . . . and sometimes it even falls out! What else changes?

God never changes. He is the same today as He was in the time of Abraham and Moses. He is still all-powerful, still loving, still all-knowing, still just, still holy, still good, still faithful . . .

For I the Lord do not change. (Malachi 3:6)

God doesn't change, so His Word doesn't change either. What God said about Himself in the Bible is still true today. His promises haven't changed. What the Bible tells us about the creation of the world and how the world will end is still right. Everything the Bible says about sin is still true today. And Jesus' death on the cross is still the way sinners come to God. Everything God has said in the Bible is still His Word, and it will not change.

Forever, O Lord, your word
   is firmly fixed in the heavens. (Psalm 119:89)

There are three very important words in this verse about the Word of God. Can you find them? They all start with the letter *f*. The important words are "forever," "firmly," and "fixed."

God's Word is *forever*. It wasn't just for Bible times. Everything God said in the Bible, He still declares today. Forever means "for all time"—not just for a little while, not just until Jesus came, not just until today, but for all time.

God's Word is *fixed*. This doesn't mean it was broken before, and now it isn't. God didn't have to correct His Word. It has always been right and true. When the Bible says God's Word is "fixed," it means tightly in place, permanent, unchanging; it can't be moved. God's Word isn't going away. It won't lose power or truth. It is unshakable and solid. Nothing is going to change it, destroy it, or take it away.

Firmly means it is not only fixed in the heavens, but it is so strongly in place that nothing can affect it, pry it loose, hide it away, make it disappear, or put something else in its place.

These are very strong words about God's Word. It is *forever firmly fixed!* So we never have to worry that God will change His Word, or that suddenly God and His ways will be different than they are now.

Do you know why it is so important that God's Word never changes? First it might be helpful to understand what happens when ways of doing things change.

Suppose your zoo has a special deal on Tuesdays. On that day, children can get in free. Only the adults need to pay. So your family of six people plans a Tuesday trip to the zoo. When you get there, the person in the ticket office tells you that you have to pay for six tickets, not two.

When you remind the ticket person that children are free on Tuesdays, she replies, "Oh, we don't do that anymore. We changed that a long time ago."

This is disappointing because it creates a problem for your family. Either you will have to decide not to go to the zoo, or you will have to spend extra money. This is a problem, but it isn't a big problem.

But if God's Word changed like the zoo's special deal changed, that would be a HUGE problem. Just imagine how terrible that would be! A Christian could face God expecting to go to heaven, and He could say, "Oh, I don't accept Jesus' death as a payment for sin anymore. I was tired of the old way and decided to change it."

God's Word says, "I will be with you always." But if the Bible was not forever firmly fixed, you could be in a really hard situation, and God might say, "Sorry. You are on your own. I don't do hard situations anymore."

Instead of being "merciful and gracious, slow to anger and abounding in steadfast love" (Psalm 103:8), God could say, "Being merciful and gracious really isn't in style anymore. I decided not to be slow to anger so I am going to wipe you off the face of the earth because of that lie you told."

But God would *never* say those things, because He is unchanging, and His Word is unchanging. It will be the same in a hundred years, or in a thousand years. You can have complete confidence in the unchanging Word of God, because it is *forever firmly fixed.*

For truly, I say to you, until heaven and earth pass away, not an iota, not a dot, will pass from the Law until all is accomplished. (Matthew 5:18)

LEARNING TO TRUST GOD

✛ Read Psalm 119:89–91. What do you see in these verses that is unchanging? How strong are the words that are used? Why does the Bible use such strong language?

✛ Read Psalm 103:8–19. Why is it good that these verses are unchanging? Thank God that His Word never changes.

✛ *Activity:* Go to a park and swing on the swings. What would happen if the poles and chains weren't "firmly fixed"? How would you feel if they weren't stable? How does having something firmly fixed affect you? Why should knowing that the Bible is forever firmly fixed in the heavens give you great confidence? Make a bookmark for your Bible with Psalm 119:89 on it. Use it as a reminder when you read your Bible that God's Word is unchanging.

God Preserves His Word

What do you know about dinosaurs? Have you ever seen a dinosaur? Can you go to a zoo and find a dinosaur? Why not?

Dinosaurs are *extinct*. This means there are no more living dinosaurs. They have all died out. They are gone for good. There will never be dinosaurs again.

Do you think the Bible will ever be extinct? In a hundred or two hundred years, will people still have a Bible to read? Will there be no more Bibles? Would God ever let His Word disappear?

The eternal living God will always have a message for His people. Other things will disappear, but God's Word will last forever.

Heaven and earth will pass away, but my words will not pass away. (Matthew 24:35)

Someday heaven and earth as we know it will be extinct. There will be a new heaven and a new earth, but the Word of God will never pass away. The words that God has spoken and the promises He has made are forever. God will also preserve the Bible. This means He will guard or protect it. He will watch over it and make sure people always have the Bible.

Evil men have tried to destroy the Bible, but they have failed because God preserves His Word.

One of these evil men was Jehoiakim. He was the King of Judah (southern Israel) in Bible times, but he did not encourage the people to worship the one true God. Jehoiakim and the people disobeyed God's command to have "no other gods," so there was much idol worship in Judah.

God will not let anyone take His place, so He sent the prophet Jeremiah to warn the people of Judah. Jeremiah warned the people that the temple and the city of Jerusalem would be destroyed, and that the people of Judah would be taken captive. He pleaded with them to turn from idols and turn back to God.

Because God wanted His words written down, Jeremiah told them to his friend Baruch, who wrote God's words on a scroll. Then, since Jeremiah was not allowed in the temple, Baruch went to the temple and read from the scroll so the people could hear the Word of God.

Some of the people were afraid of the warning, so they brought the scroll to King Jehoiakim. When the scroll was read to Jehoiakim, he was furious! He was so angry that he cut the scroll of God's Word into pieces and threw them into the fire! He would put an end to God's Word!

He also decided to put an end to Jeremiah and Baruch, so that they could never write these words again! He ordered Jeremiah and Baruch to be taken as his prisoners, but they couldn't be found. God had hidden them away so that a new scroll could be written. Jehoiakim could not get rid of God's Word. Other things can be destroyed forever, but God watches over His Word and preserves it so all people in all times can know Him.

Jehoiakim was not the only person who thought that he could get rid of the Word of God. About 900 years later, Diocletian, a Roman emperor who was an idol worshipper, ordered that all Bibles be burned. He also tore down churches and threw religious leaders in prison. He proudly thought he had destroyed Christianity. He even had a medal engraved with the words, "The Christian religion is destroyed." But Diocletian was wrong. God watches over His Word and preserves it.

About 1400 years after Diocletian, a French writer named Voltaire boasted that before 100 years passed, the Bible would disappear. Has that happened? No, it hasn't happened, and it never will happen because God preserves His Word. Voltaire has died . . . but God's Word is still living!

God is spreading His Word around the world. God does not hide from us. He wants all peoples everywhere to have His Word and to know Him. The Bible is in more languages today than at any other time in history.[1] God's Word is not disappearing!

The grass withers, the flower fades,
> but the word of our God will stand forever. (Isaiah 40:8)

1. According to Wycliffe Bible Translators, the entire Bible has been translated into more than 500 languages, and there are parts of the Bible translated into all but 2,000 of the 6,800+ languages of the world ("Why Bible Translation?", *Wycliffe*, accessed November 4, 2014, http://www.wycliffe.org/about/why).

LEARNING TO TRUST GOD

✢ Read Jeremiah 36:27–32; 2 Chronicles 36:5–6. What do these passages tell you about the Word of God? Thank God for what He did to preserve His Word for you.

✢ Read Isaiah 40:6–8 and explain it to your mother or father.

✢ *Activity:* Your copy of the Bible won't last forever, but God's Word will last forever. He will make sure that there are always Bibles. But it is good to take care of your Bible. How can you take care of it? How can you mark in it neatly? Make or buy a cover for your Bible, or read about Bible translation.[2] How can your family pray for or give toward Bible translation? Make a plan and follow it.

2. Information is found at http://www.wycliffe.org/.

The Bible Is Powerful

Have you ever wished you could just say something and it would happen? What would you say? Would you say, "Room, be clean!" or "Ice cream sundae, appear!"? Wouldn't that be great! But that really doesn't happen . . . or does it?

It doesn't happen for us, but it does happen for God. God is all-powerful, so His words are powerful—both the words He speaks and His words in the Bible.

Do you remember how God created the world? He just spoke . . . and the world was created! He said, "Let there be light," and there was light. God spoke, and the sun, moon, and stars were created. God said, "Let the earth bring forth living creatures," and there were horses and dogs, alligators and frogs, cows and hogs. God's Word is powerful. It created the whole world.

Jesus and His disciples were in a boat on the sea when a big storm came. The disciples were afraid, but Jesus just stood up and said, "Peace! Be still!" All Jesus did was speak, and the wind and the waves stopped! Everything was calm. God's word is powerful! Even the winds and the waves obey the word of God.

But God's Word is also powerful in another way. His Word has the power to change hearts. It can show people their sin and cause them to repent or turn away from their sin. This is what God's Word did in David's heart.

David loved God, but David still had a sin nature, and one day he sinned terribly. He took another man's wife and treated her like his own wife. Then he had the man killed! This made God angry and sad. What David did was very wrong.

But God loved David. So He sent the prophet Nathan to speak for Him. Nathan brought God's Word to David by telling a story about two men. One man was rich and had many sheep and cattle. The other one was poor and had only one little lamb.

The poor man took good care of the lamb. It was like a pet. The lamb grew up with the man's children. It shared the man's food, drank from his cup, and even slept in his arms.

One day the rich man had a guest. The rich man didn't want to take one of his many sheep or cows to serve for supper. So instead he took the one little lamb that belonged to the poor man; he stole it, and he and his guest ate it for dinner!

The story made David angry! He said to Nathan,

As the LORD lives, the man who has done this deserves to die, and he shall restore the lamb fourfold, because he did this thing, and because he had no pity. (2 Samuel 12:5–6)

Do you know what Nathan said to David? He said, "You are the man!" God's story was really about David and his sin in taking another man's wife.

What do you think David did when Nathan's words pointed to him? He didn't get angry at Nathan or lie about his sin. God's Word is powerful, and it went deep into David's heart. He knew it was the truth. He knew He had sinned against the God who had been so good to him. He knew what he had done was evil.

David said to Nathan, "I have sinned against the LORD." (2 Samuel 12:13)

God did not shake David by the shoulders or beat him. God's Word was powerful. It was enough to show David his sin and how awful it was. David loved God and truly wanted to please God, so when God's Word showed David his sin, David was grieved.

God's Word always does what God sends it to do. Just as God sends rain for a purpose—to water the earth—so He sends His Word for a purpose too. Sometimes that purpose is to change a person's heart. God's Word does not fail, no matter what, because it is always powerful.

But sometimes God's Word has another purpose. What did Jehoiakim, in our last story, do when he heard God's Word? Did he repent like David? Did God's Word change his heart? No, it didn't. Jehoiakim tore up God's Word and threw it in the fire! God did not send His Word to change Jehoiakim's heart. Jehoiakim was an evil man, and God sent His Word of warning so that when God punished Jehoiakim he would know that God's Word is powerful and true. Jehoiakim was captured, and his kingdom ended just like God's Word said it would.

Do you read God's powerful Word? What happens in your heart when you read the Bible? Do you hear God's Word and respond with a soft heart like David, or do you turn away from God's Word with a hard heart like Jehoiakim?

For as the rain and the snow come down from heaven
    and do not return there but water the earth,

making it bring forth and sprout,
     giving seed to the sower and bread to the eater,
so shall my word be that goes out from my mouth;
     it shall not return to me empty,
but it shall accomplish that which I purpose,
     and shall succeed in the thing for which I sent it. (Isaiah 55:10–11)

LEARNING TO TRUST GOD

✦ Read Isaiah 55:10–11 again. Explain it to your mom or dad. Then put the verse in your own words.

✦ Read 2 Samuel 12:1–15. Where do you see God's goodness and God's justice in this story? Where do you see the power of God's Word? How does David's response show a soft heart? How would a person with a hard heart respond to God's message through Nathan? Is there sin you need to repent of? Ask God to give you a soft heart.

✦ *Activity:* How can your family bring God's powerful Word to someone else? Write a card, have a conversation, show a Christian film, sing a hymn or praise song, or bring God's Word to someone in another way. Trust God to use His powerful Word to accomplish His purposes.

The Bible Is the Authority

Could you decide to change the name of your street, or what time your grocery store will open? Why not? You're not in charge of those things. If you want permission to play at a friend's house, who makes the decision whether you can go? Why can't you just decide to go?

Only the person in charge of something can decide about it. The person in charge is the one who has the right to make the rules. That person is the "authority" or the "boss." A teacher is the authority—the one in charge—of a classroom. The police are in charge of making sure people keep the law. And your parents are in charge over you.

But who is the greatest authority, the boss of the whole world, the one in charge of all things? God is the highest authority. He created the world and everything in it, so He owns everything. He has the right to decide what He wants to do with His world, and He makes the rules for all the people in the world. What God says is the way it is. He is in charge of all things and His Word is the authority over all things.

Suppose a king decides to build a bridge for the people of his country. When the bridge is done, the king makes a law or a rule for everyone using his bridge. Anyone who wants to cross the bridge has to pay a fee of one dollar.

Can an ordinary person decide to change the king's law? Can he decide that the cost will be fifty cents, or that the bridge is free on Saturday and Sunday? No, the king's word is the final word. What the king says is the way it is, and no one has the right or the authority to change the king's order.

God is the King of the whole world, and He has laws, too. If someone does not like something in the Bible, does he have the right to change it, or to ignore or disobey it? No, what the Bible says is the way it is.

> You have commanded your precepts
> to be kept diligently. (Psalm 119:4)

God's laws and His ways are good for us because God made us, and He knows what is best for us. He has put His ways, His laws, and His decisions in His Word. How happy it should make us that God loves us enough to show us the best way to live!

I will delight in your statutes;
   I will not forget your word. (Psalm 119:16)

Many people will tell you things about God, the world, and man. Some of these things will be true, and some won't be. How will you know? God in perfect

wisdom wrote the Bible. So we can trust the Bible. The way to know if something is true is to see what the Bible has to say about it.

If someone tells you the world was started by a big accident, should you believe it? How would you answer that person? The Bible has the true answers. It is God's perfect Word of truth, and everything God says is right, because He is in charge and He knows all things. What does the Bible tell us about the how the world started?

In the beginning, God created the heavens and the earth. (Genesis 1:1)

That is the truth, because that is what God says!

How would you answer someone who says, "There is more than one God"? Would you believe him or would you know that it is not true? What does the Bible say?

I am God, and there is no other;
  I am God, and there is none like me. (Isaiah 46:9)

What if a friend tells you, "You don't have to obey your parents all the time. It is okay to watch this movie they told you not to watch. They will never know." How would you answer him? What does the Bible say?

Children, obey your parents in the Lord, for this is right. (Ephesians 6:1)

God is the greatest authority, and the Bible is God's Word of truth. No one has the right to change what God says. Only God's Word is the perfect Word of truth. Only God's Word has the authority over what is right and what is wrong. God gave us His perfect Word because He loves us.

I will delight in your statutes;
  I will not forget your word. (Psalm 119:16)

LEARNING TO TRUST GOD

✤ Read Psalm 119:1–6. What is the writer's attitude toward God's law? Why does a person want to obey God's Word?

✤ Read Romans 1:18–21. What do these verses tell you about why someone would want to change what God says or disobey God's Word?

✤ *Activity:* Play "What if someone tells you . . . ?" Say something untrue that someone might say, and then find the true answer in the Bible. Thank God for His love shown toward us by giving us the truth.

The Bible Gives Hope

What's your favorite Bible story? Is it the story about God opening the Red Sea, or the one about the walls of Jericho tumbling down? Maybe it's God rescuing Jonah with a big fish, or Jesus quieting the storm? Why are all these stories in the Bible?

The Bible says,

For whatever was written in former days was written for our instruction. (Romans 15:4)

The Bible is full of stories about the things God did for His people. These were written to teach us something. They teach us about God as they show us His mighty acts. Just think of the amazing things God did for His people!

- Abraham had no son. BUT GOD gave him a son in his old age.
- Joseph was thrown into a pit, made a slave in Egypt, and then put in jail. BUT GOD made him second in charge in Egypt and used him to rescue His people from famine.
- The Hebrew boys were being killed in Egypt. BUT GOD rescued Moses, and through him led His people out of slavery.
- The Israelites were facing the Red Sea on one side and the Egyptian armies on the other. BUT GOD opened the sea and led them through on dry land.
- There was no food in the wilderness for the people of God. BUT GOD sent manna from heaven, blew quail in on the wind, and brought water out of a rock.
- The land of Canaan was filled with well-protected, walled cities and the enemies of Israel. BUT GOD gave them victory over their enemies.

- We deserve eternal punishment for our sin. BUT GOD sent His Son to save us from our sins.

Time after time, things looked hopeless for the people of Israel, but God worked for His people. The Bible is full of "BUT GODs." God has been faithful to His people throughout all of history. All of the "BUT GOD" times in the Bible are written for us to learn that we can have great hope in God.

For whatever was written in former days was written for our instruction, that through endurance . . . (Romans 15:4)

What does "endurance" mean? Endurance is "hanging on." It is sticking to something and not giving up. Maybe an example will help you to understand about endurance.

Suppose you are hiking with two friends, and you slip and fall over a cliff. As you are falling, you are able to grab a branch growing out from the side of the cliff. You are hanging in midair and can't crawl back up the cliff.

One friend runs for help. The other understands that

if you let go of the branch, you will fall and be seriously hurt. He stands at the top of the cliff calling encouraging words to you: "Hang on. Help is coming. God will help you. I know you can do it. It won't be much longer."

Your muscles are so tired that they start to burn. Your hands ache. But you keep holding on to the branch. You are determined not to let go. This is endurance. Endurance is holding on to the branch even when it's hard and you feel like giving up. It means hanging on and not letting go.

When the Bible talks about endurance, it means hanging on to the promises of God. It means believing that God is faithful and is working for you. It means not giving up hoping in God, even when things look bad.

How can we have endurance and not give up hoping in God? God has given us Bible verses to encourage us. They give us hope and confidence that God will work for our good.

> For whatever was written in former days was written for our instruction, that through endurance and through the encouragement of the Scriptures we might have hope. (Romans 15:4)

The Bible is all about hope—and the good reasons for our hope. The "encouragement of the Scriptures" is like the friend calling down to us from the top of the cliff. They encourage us to keep believing in God and to know that He is at work for us. The words of hope from the Bible are verses like:

> God is our refuge and strength,
>   a very present help in trouble. (Psalm 46:1)

> Weeping may tarry for the night,
>   but joy comes with the morning. (Psalm 30:5)

For I know the plans I have for you, declares the LORD, plans for welfare and not for evil, to give you a future and a hope. (Jeremiah 29:11)

What other words of encouragement from the Bible do you know?

No matter what happens to you, no matter how bad things may look, Christians always have a reason to hope in God. Things may *look* hopeless . . . BUT GOD . . . !

LEARNING TO TRUST GOD

✤ Read a story from the Bible and look for the "BUT GOD" part of the story. What does this tell you about God? Can you think of a "BUT GOD" story in the life of your family?

✤ Make a list of at least ten verses of encouragement. How do these verses teach you to hope in God?

✤ *Activity:* There are many discouraged people who need to be reminded to hope in God. With your family, write an encouraging note for someone who needs encouragement using one of your ten verses. Mail or deliver it with a special treat or small gift.

The Bible Protects from Sin

Suppose a batter is waiting for the next pitch. The pitcher throws the ball, and the batter's teammates start yelling to him. One person yells, "Don't swing!" But the rest of the team and some of the fans yell loudly, "Swing! Swing! Hit the ball! Swing!" What do you think the batter would more likely do? He would probably listen to all the people telling him to swing at the ball . . . even if they are wrong.

Very often, we listen to the "loudest and most repeated" suggestions. We hear them so often that they are hard to ignore. They affect the way we think, and what we think affects what we do. That is why we must be careful about what we put into our minds.

> How can a young man keep his way pure?
>   By guarding it according to your word.
> With my whole heart I seek you;
>   let me not wander from your commandments!
> I have stored up your word in my heart,
>   that I might not sin against you. (Psalm 119:9–11)

God tells us good and right things over and over in His Word. So reading the Bible protects us from sin by filling our thoughts and hearts with what is right. But if we do not fill our hearts and minds with the goodness of God's Word, we will more likely follow the sinful ways of this world. We will not be able to trust God when things are hard or to believe His promises. This is what happened to the ten spies. Do you know the story?

Moses sent twelve spies to check out the land of Canaan. After forty days, the spies returned to tell Moses and the people of Israel what they saw. They said the land was just like God said it was . . . but the people were strong, and the cities were well protected. There were many voices talking about the strong people living in the land—loud, repeated voices of fear and doubt.

Were the strong people and the well-protected cities a problem for God? No! Caleb knew this. So he "quieted the people" and said,

> Let us go up at once and occupy it, for we are well able to overcome it. (Numbers 13:30)

Caleb had his mind on the greatness of God. He knew God would help the people of Israel, just like He had helped His people in the past.

> Then the men who had gone up with him said, "We are not able to go up against the people, for they are stronger than we are." (Numbers 13:31)

They repeated the dangers they saw. They were not thinking of the greatness of God. They could think only about how strong the people were. The people of Israel cried aloud. They were so afraid that they wanted to go back to Egypt! While so many of them were complaining, crying, and not trusting God, Joshua and Caleb tried to remind them of who God is. They said,

> If the LORD delights in us, he will bring us into this land and give it to us, a land that flows with milk and honey. Only do not rebel against the LORD. And do not fear the people of the land, for they are bread for us. Their protection is removed from them, and the LORD is with us; do not fear them. (Numbers 14:8–9)

But the people listened to the repeated words of fear from the ten spies instead of the words of trust in God from Joshua and Caleb. They did not put in their minds the goodness or power or faithfulness of God. They sinned against God by not trusting Him, and they spent forty years wandering in the wilderness because of their sin.

Remembering God's mighty acts, His faithfulness, and His goodness that we read about in the Bible keeps us from sin. The Bible protects our minds and our hearts. It is like a raincoat.

A raincoat? How is the Bible like a raincoat?

Have you ever been caught in a heavy rainstorm? What were you wearing? How wet did you get? If you had boots and a raincoat, you probably stayed pretty dry. Boots and raincoats are a protection against getting wet.

The Word of God is like the raincoat and boots. It is a protection for us against sin. It helps us to guard our hearts and our minds from the wrong suggestions that we hear repeatedly. It tells us what is right to do and shows us that we can trust God.

Suppose you broke a vase while throwing a ball in the house. How could the Bible protect you? When your mother asks you if you broke the vase, you might be tempted to lie. But if you have the Word of God in your mind and heart, it will tell you what is right.

Do not lie to one another, seeing that you have put off the old self with its practices. (Colossians 3:9)

God's Word is good and right. It can protect you from sin . . . but only if you know the Word. A raincoat won't protect you in a rainstorm if you don't have a raincoat, or if you have one and don't use it. And God's Word won't protect you if you do not read the Bible and know God's ways, warnings, and promises. If you don't know the mighty acts of God, you will have a hard time trusting God.

What are you putting into your mind? Do you put the Word of God into your mind every day? Do you have verses memorized that can protect you from sin? How can you put more of God's Word into your mind?

This Book of the Law shall not depart from your mouth, but you shall meditate on it day and night, so that you may be careful to do according to all that is written in it. For then you will make your way prosperous, and then you will have good success. (Joshua 1:8)

LEARNING TO TRUST GOD

+ Read about Israel's failure to trust God in Numbers 13:25–14:25. What should the people have remembered about the Lord? What was the consequence of their sin?

+ Find two or three Bible verses to memorize that can help you trust God and can be a protection against sin. Work on memorizing them over the next few weeks.

+ *Activity:* Read Psalm 119:11 again. Are you storing up God's Word in your heart? What can you do to store up less of the world's words and more of God's words in your heart? Make a plan with your family and put it into practice.

The Bible Is a Guide

Have you ever seen a guide dog for a blind person? The dog is specially trained to stop at curbs and stairs, to avoid obstacles, and to guide the blind person safely. Since the blind person can't see barriers or dangers, he could have an accident without the help of the dog. But if he trusts the guide dog to lead him, he will be safe.

The Bible is much like the guide dog, and we are like the blind person. Often we don't know what to do, or what decision to make, or what is right. We are blind. But like the faithful guide dog, the Bible is a trustworthy guide. The Bible always points us in the right direction. It is like a light in the darkness.

> Your word is a lamp to my feet
>   and a light to my path. (Psalm 119:105)

Have you ever been on a dark path, maybe when camping, or at a cabin in the woods far away from the city lights? It is sometimes so dark that you can't even see the path. But a flashlight or a lantern can put light on the path so you know where to go.

The Bible is like a light on a dark path. It shows us what is true and teaches us what is right and wrong. The Bible always has good instruction for us. If we depend on the Bible for understanding, instead of thinking we know all the answers, we will be wise.

> Your testimonies are my delight;
>   they are my counselors. (Psalm 119:24)

When Jesus was in the wilderness, Satan tried to make Him do the wrong thing. But Jesus knew what was right because He knew the Word of God. He delighted in God's Word, and it was His "counselor" or guide. So He knew just how to answer Satan.

Satan knew Jesus was hungry, so he tempted Jesus to turn stones into loaves of bread. He wanted Jesus to obey him and follow his suggestion. But Jesus answered him,

It is written,

"Man shall not live by bread alone,
  but by every word that comes from the mouth of God." (Matthew 4:4)

The Bible was His guide. It showed Him what is true.

Then Satan told Jesus to throw Himself down from a high place because God would send angels to help Jesus. But the Word of God guided Jesus.

Jesus said to him, "Again it is written, 'You shall not put the Lord your God to the test.'" (Matthew 4:7)

Satan even promised to give Jesus all the kingdoms of the world if Jesus would worship him. Did Jesus follow the wicked suggestion of Satan? No! Once again, the Word of God was His counselor.

Then Jesus said to him, "Be gone, Satan! For it is written,

> 'You shall worship the Lord your God
>   and him only shall you serve.'" (Matthew 4:10)

Every time Satan tempted Jesus, Jesus answered, "It is written . . ." He knew just what to do each time because the Bible was His counselor and guide.

There are many "loud and repeated voices" in our world. Some are truthful, but many are lies or wicked suggestions like the following:

- There is no God.
- You don't have to tell the truth all the time. A little lie is no big deal. Everyone does it. No one will know anyway.
- Your friends know more than your parents do. You don't have to listen to your parents.
- A few bad scenes in a movie won't hurt you.
- The Bible is boring. You don't have to listen during family devotions or church.
- A woman has a right to have an abortion if she wants it. It's not a baby.
- A person can marry anyone he wants.

Without a light, a person walking on a dark path is pretty sure to stumble and fall. And without the Word of God, you will not know what is true and what is untrue. How can you keep from listening to lies and wicked suggestions? How can you keep from stumbling and falling into sin and great sorrow?

The Bible always shows us what is right. It is the only completely trustworthy guide. Do you know what it says? Are you ready to answer the many voices rightly?

> Incline your ear, and hear the words of the wise,
>   and apply your heart to my knowledge,

for it will be pleasant if you keep them within you,
    if all of them are ready on your lips.
That your trust may be in the LORD. (Proverbs 22:17–19)

LEARNING TO TRUST GOD

✛ Read Proverbs 22:17–19. Then explain it to your mother or father.

✛ Read Matthew 4:1–11. How was the Bible Jesus' guide? Did Satan go away the first time Jesus resisted him? What can you learn from this story?

✛ *Activity:* With your family, take turns being blindfolded and led by someone else. What does it mean to trust the person guiding you? What must you do? How trustworthy is the person guiding you? How do you know that the Bible is a trustworthy guide? Look at the list of lies and wicked suggestions above. What guidance does the Bible give you about these statements? Pray and ask God to give you a love for His Word and the obedience to follow it.

Satan Tries to Keep Us from the Bible

What takes up your time? Does your list include going to school, eating, sleeping, taking music lessons, playing sports, practicing, attending parties or family gatherings, keeping appointments to the doctor or dentist, completing chores, going to church, watching television, reading, and playing games?

All these things keep us very busy. Sometimes they keep us too busy. Sometimes we are so busy that we don't take time to read the Bible. Is that a good choice? Even though other things are important, what is more important than spending time with God?

Martha was busy too. She was busy making and serving a meal. She had invited Jesus to her house and wanted to give Him a nice meal. She had a lot to do because her sister Mary wasn't helping her.

Do you know what Mary was doing? She wasn't rushing around, thinking about the meal. She was listening to Jesus. She wanted to hear what Jesus was teaching about God. She wanted to be with her friend Jesus.

This made Martha upset. Why wasn't her sister helping her with the meal? So Mary complained to Jesus. She wanted Him to tell Mary to help her. But Jesus didn't tell Mary to help Martha. Instead, He told Martha that listening to Him was the better choice.

What Martha was doing was important. It was a good thing to do. But it wasn't the best thing to do. The very best thing to do was to sit and listen to Jesus, to enjoy being with Him, and to learn from Him—like Mary was doing.

Do you know that often we are too much like Martha and not enough like Mary? We can choose to spend time with Jesus. We can pray to Him and read

His words in the Bible. Or we can choose to do other things, which may be good and even important things. But these things are not as important as being with Jesus and reading His Word.

Many times the desires of our own hearts pull us away from reading the Bible. We want to do other things instead of reading the Bible. Sometimes we don't read the Bible because we just don't make it important enough to us. We let other things take up our time. So we need to plan a *time* to read the Bible.

Time: Choose a time when you will read your Bible each day. Sometimes early in the morning is the best time—before you get busy doing other things.

Sometimes when we do start to read the Bible or pray, we let other things take our attention away from the Bible. We start to think about other things, or we start to do something else. So the next step is to plan a *place* for reading the Bible.

Place: Find a quiet place without things around to pull your attention away from reading the Bible and praying.

But we have another problem. Do you know what it is? The other problem is that Satan doesn't want us to read the Bible. He fights against us when we try to read the Bible or pray. He tempts us to start doing something else. Or he tempts us to think about something else so we won't pay attention or think about what we are reading in the Bible. He does not want us to do anything that will help us to know God better.

Satan hates God. He is God's enemy, and he is our enemy. Do you know how the Bible describes him?

Be sober-minded; be watchful. Your adversary the devil prowls around like a roaring lion, seeking someone to devour. (1 Peter 5:8)

Why do you think the Bible says Satan is like a lion? Lions are strong and they sneak around ready to eat whatever they find. Satan is a strong and clever enemy—but God is so much *stronger* and so much *smarter* than Satan. God is always ready to help His children when they ask Him. The most important thing we can do in fighting against Satan is to *pray*.

Pray: Ask God to give you a desire to read His Word. Ask Him to help you fight against Satan and concentrate on what you are reading. Ask Him to speak to you through His Word.

What do you do when Satan tries to distract you with other thoughts or desires? You *resist* him immediately.

Resist: Tell Satan, "No!" Refuse to follow his suggestions.

If you find a *time* and a *place*, and if you *pray*, asking God to help you, and *resist* Satan, you will find wonderful stories of God's mighty acts in the Bible. You will discover what is true, and you will have a guide to show you what is right. You will have protection from sin. And, best of all, you will begin to know God.

> Blessed is the man
> who walks not in the counsel of the wicked,
> nor stands in the way of sinners,
> nor sits in the seat of scoffers;
> but his delight is in the law of the LORD,
> and on his law he meditates day and night. (Psalm 1:1–2)

LEARNING TO TRUST GOD

✠ Read James 4:7. What does "submit" mean? What does "resist" mean? How can you resist Satan? What promise is in this verse?

✠ Read Psalm 1. Why is reading the Bible such a blessing? What attitude do we need to read the Bible daily? (Hint: see verse 2.) Can you make yourself delight in the Bible? Ask God to give you a delight in His Word and to help you resist Satan.

✠ *Activity:* With your family, find a time and place for your Bible reading. Are there distractions you need to remove? Then make a plan for what you will do in your Bible time. Be sure not to miss a blessing by neglecting to read your Bible every day.

The Bible Was Written So That You May Believe

Some people really like raisins. But others don't like raisins at all. Which kind of person are you? The reason some people like raisins and others don't is not because of the raisins. Raisins are raisins. They are the same raisins for both kinds of people. The difference is in the people—some are raisin-lovers, and some are raisin-haters.

Just as there are people who like raisins and people who do not like them, there are also people who love and believe in Jesus and people who do not love and believe in Jesus. Jesus is still the same Jesus. The difference is in how people respond to Jesus.

Can you think of some people the Bible tells us about who loved and trusted Jesus? Maybe you thought of Peter or John, Mary or Lazarus, or Stephen or Timothy. How about Judas? He didn't love Jesus at all—even though he knew Jesus well. His heart was hard.

The Bible also tells us about two criminals—men who broke the law. They had both done something very wrong. What they did was so bad that they were hung on a cross to die. These were the two men who hung on either side of Jesus when He was crucified.

One criminal made fun of Jesus. He was disrespectful and did not believe that Jesus is God. He was not sorry for what he had done. But the second criminal feared God. He knew that what he did was wrong, and he was afraid of God's punishment for his sin.

The second criminal also knew something else. He knew that Jesus hadn't done anything wrong. He knew that he and the other criminal both deserved to die on a cross but that Jesus was innocent and didn't deserve to be killed. This man treated Jesus with respect and understood that Jesus is the Son of God. He knew Jesus has the power to forgive sin.

Do you know what this criminal asked Jesus?

Jesus, remember me when you come into your kingdom. (Luke 23:42)

What kingdom was the man talking about? He was talking about heaven. He truly believed that after Jesus died on the cross, Jesus would reign as king in heaven.

Why would Jesus remember this criminal? He was a sinner who had broken the law. Why should Jesus even pay attention to him or care about him? But this is how Jesus answered him:

Truly, I say to you, today you will be with me in Paradise. (Luke 23:43)

Jesus welcomes all who come to Him—even criminals! Jesus is happy when sinners turn from sin. That is why Jesus came to earth—to save sinners who trust in Him. So Jesus gladly received this criminal who believed in Him.

What about the other man? Jesus did not promise to remember him or receive him into heaven. Jesus does not welcome people who do not turn from sin and believe in Him.

Jesus was the same Jesus to both criminals. He did not change. He is God and has the power to forgive sins and welcome sinners. Both criminals saw the same Jesus, but they treated Him differently. One man trusted Jesus; the other didn't. One man honored Jesus; the other didn't. One man believed and went to heaven; the other died in his sin and could not enter heaven.

Why do you think this story about the two criminals is in the Bible? Why does the Bible tell us about the flood, the opening of the Red Sea, and the walls of Jericho? Why do we need to know that Jesus healed blind eyes and lame legs, calmed the wind and waves, and raised Lazarus from the dead?

God knew we would ask these questions, and He gave us this answer in the book of John:

Now Jesus did many other signs in the presence of the disciples, which are not written in this book; but these are written so that you may believe that Jesus is the Christ, the Son of God, and that by believing you may have life in his name. (John 20:30–31)

God wants us to know Him. He wants us to know that He is the Almighty God. He wants us to know that He is powerful, loving, all-knowing, and unchanging. He wants us to know that He is the answer to our sin problem. The Bible is His message to us. He preserves or watches over His Word so that all peoples in all times can know and believe in Him and can trust in Jesus' work on the cross.

You can know God and trust in Jesus as your Savior. In the precious Word of God you can find everything you need to know to believe in Jesus.

So faith comes from hearing, and hearing through the word of Christ. (Romans 10:17)

LEARNING TO TRUST GOD

✛ Read John 20:30–31 again. Explain it to your mother or father.

✛ Read Acts 8:26–38. How did the Ethiopian come to believe in Jesus?

✛ *Activity:* Just as God used His Word and the testimony of Philip to lead the Ethiopian to faith, so God can use His Word and your family in the life of a person who doesn't know Him. How can your family be God's messengers to bring His Word to someone else? Do something this week to share the Bible with someone.

Being a Doer and Not Just a Hearer

Sparky is a sea lion who lives at the Como Zoo in St. Paul, Minnesota. A sea lion is like a seal. Every summer, Sparky performs tricks in front of an audience. Sparky's trainer gives voice and hand commands, and Sparky obeys them. Sparky performs tricks like clapping her flippers, catching balls, blowing a trumpet, and jumping through a hoop. How do you think the trainer teaches Sparky these tricks?

The trainer knows that Sparky loves to eat fish, so she uses fish to train Sparky. When Sparky obeys a command, she is rewarded with a tasty raw fish! She obeys because she loooooooooooooves fish!

Just like Sparky's obedience comes from her love for fish, our obedience should come from love too. Jesus said,

If you love me, you will keep my commandments. (John 14:15)

Jesus is saying that obedience to His commands comes from our love for Him. If we love Him, we will obey Him. So if we don't obey God's commands, perhaps we don't truly love Him. We don't trust Him, or don't believe that His ways are right and good. Obedience is a sign that we truly do have faith.

Faith by itself, if it does not have works, is dead. . . . You believe that God is one; you do well. Even the demons believe—and shudder! (James 2:17, 19)

True saving faith, true belief in and love for Jesus, is shown by following His commands. Just to *say* that we believe in Jesus doesn't mean that we truly love and trust Him. Even Satan believes that God is real, but it isn't a trusting, obeying, saving faith. Truly believing in someone means having enough faith and confidence in what he says that you *do* what he tells you to do.

Suppose two children are standing at the side of a pool. Because they can't swim, they are afraid of the water. But their dad says to each of them, one at a time, "Jump, and I will catch you." One child looks at his dad and jumps into the water. The other stands at the side of the pool and cries, refusing to move. Which child do you think truly believes that his dad will catch him?

Both children would probably say they trust their dad. But only one had true deep trust. His trust was shown by his obedience. The other child says he trusts, but does he truly trust his dad? His fear of water is greater than his trust of his father. Do you know what the Bible says about him? The Bible says that he is "deceiving" himself.

> But be doers of the word, and not hearers only, deceiving yourselves (James 1:22)

To be "deceived" means to be fooled. It is thinking something that isn't true. The boy thinks he trusts his father, but he really does not trust his dad enough to obey him.

The Bible says that if we read the Bible but don't follow God's teaching in it, we are deceived—we are fooled into thinking that we have faith when we really don't.

When the Bible says, "Don't lie and don't steal," it doesn't mean "If you feel like it, don't lie and don't steal." When the Bible tells us to be kind to one another, it doesn't say, "Be kind if it isn't too much trouble to be kind." When the Bible tells us to do something, we are to do it. True faith is trusting God and acting on what He says because we know His ways are good and right. If we don't obey, we are only hearers and not doers.

God told Abram to leave his home and travel to a faraway country where God would bless him and make him the father of many nations. What did Abram do? Did he truly believe God's promise? Was he a "doer" or a "hearer" only?

Abram obeyed God and left his home. He was a doer of the Word. His obedience showed that he had true faith in God.

Do you remember the story of the twelve spies? Most of them were hearers only. They heard about the mighty acts of God and knew His promises. But did they truly believe that God would give them the land of Canaan as He had promised? Did they go in and take the land? Ten of them were hearers only.

They were afraid to take the land. They wanted to go back to Egypt. They did not believe that God would give them victory. They did not truly believe God's Word or trust Him.

But Joshua and Caleb were not just hearers of the Word. They were doers also. They were ready to go and take the land! They believed God's promise and were ready to "jump in the water," knowing that God would catch them.

A doer of the Word obeys God because he loves God. He does not want to offend the God he loves. He trusts God and all His promises. He truly knows that God's ways are best and bring the greatest joy. He hates sin and knows that the consequences of disobedience are painful.

The Bible tells us about many people who were hearers only, and about some people who were hearers *and* doers. Churches also have hearers only and real doers. Which are you? Are you a hearer only, or a hearer *and* a doer of the Word? Do you truly love God?

If anyone loves me, he will keep my word, and my Father will love him, and we will come to him and make our home with him. (John 14:23)

LEARNING TO TRUST GOD

✛ Read James 1:22–25. Explain the difference between a hearer and a doer. What does this verse say is the result of obedience? How were you a doer of the Word this week?

✛ Read James 2:14–26. Explain these verses. Are you saved by faith or by works? What is the place of works?

✛ *Activity:* Read James 2:15-16 again. What point are these verses making? Does your family know of someone in need? How can you be a blessing to this person? Go and act in faith.

The Bible Is a Treasure

If your house was on fire and you could only grab two or three things, what would you grab? Why would you rescue these things?

Some people might say that they would grab a photo album. A photo album is full of precious memories. It reminds us of special times and dear friends, funny moments and important events, family vacations and holidays with relatives. Those memories can be relived time and again by looking at the pictures. So photo albums or pictures are precious things.

Just like a photo album, the Bible can remind us of special times with the Lord, promises that you treasure, and familiar verses that bring comfort. A Bible you have read for a long time may have favorite verses underlined, dates recorded when you were strengthened by a particular promise, or notes in the margin about what God has taught you.

A Bible like this is a special Bible. It is the precious Word of God, which is true, understandable, powerful, and unchanging. But it is also *your* Bible, your record of precious times spent with Jesus and years of walking with Him.

As you flip through the pages of a well-used Bible, you may see precious verses underlined or starred. Verses like:

Weeping may tarry for the night,
> but joy comes with the morning. (Psalm 30:5)

The steadfast love of the LORD never ceases;
> his mercies never come to an end;
they are new every morning;
> great is your faithfulness. (Lamentations 3:22–23)

And we know that for those who love God all things work together for good, for those who are called according to his purpose. (Romans 8:28)

Fear not, for I am with you;
    be not dismayed, for I am your God;
I will strengthen you, I will help you,
    I will uphold you with my righteous right hand. (Isaiah 41:10)

But to all who did receive him, who believed in his name, he gave the right to become children of God. (John 1:12)

But God shows his love for us in that while we were still sinners, Christ died for us. (Romans 5:8)

These are verses that have comforted, encouraged, and strengthened God's people for generations. God's Word gives hope and guidance and protects us from sin. These are verses from the precious Word of God that make the Bible precious to us.

Do you have a verse that is precious to you? When did it become a favorite verse?

We read many verses many times and they are good verses, but they aren't *ours* yet. They are not precious to us yet. A verse becomes precious when God causes that verse to sink down deep into our heart. Maybe you are going through a really hard time and you are discouraged. Then God touches your soul through a verse—a verse that you know is just for you for this hard time. This verse encourages you, and you think about it for days and sometimes weeks. You memorize this verse, and every time you think of the verse, your faith is encouraged. This is now *your* verse—a message to your soul from the living God.

The precious Word of God can be a book on your shelf, or it can be a personal message to you from your heavenly Father. If you know Jesus as your Savior, if you truly believe in Him as a doer of the Word, then His Word is precious to you. The Bible gives you more comfort than anything else. It encourages you, strengthens your faith, convicts you of sin, and protects you from the enemy.

The Bible is precious . . . is it precious to you?

Your words were found, and I ate them,
    and your words became to me a joy
    and the delight of my heart,
for I am called by your name,
    O LORD, God of hosts. (Jeremiah 15:16)

LEARNING TO TRUST GOD

✦ Ask your mother or father to share some of their favorite verses with you. How did these verses come to be personally applied to their lives?

✦ Talk to your mother or father about how you can make your Bible a personal record of your time with God. What ideas do you have about marking meaningful verses or writing in your Bible? How can you treat your Bible with respect while still making it personal to you?

✦ *Activity:* Have a treasure hunt, making the Bible the treasure. Mom or Dad could hide the Bible in a special gift box and make clues leading you to the Bible. When you find it, talk about why it is a treasure. Rejoice in God's goodness to give us a Bible, thanking Him for His precious Word. Then have a special treat to celebrate finishing *God's Word*.

Praying for Yourself and Those You Love Each Day

Pastor John Piper prays for people he loves by remembering verses starting with **IOUS.**[1] You, too, may want to use this tool each day to pray for yourself and others.

I: Incline my heart to your testimonies, and not to selfish gain! (Psalm 119:36).

O: Open my eyes, that I may behold wondrous things out of your law (Psalm 119:18).

U: Teach me your way, O LORD, that I may walk in your truth; **unite** my heart to fear your name (Psalm 86:11).

S: Satisfy us in the morning with your steadfast love, that we may rejoice and be glad all our days (Psalm 90:14).

Reading Your Bible Each Day

The Bible is the precious Word of God, but the enemy fights our desire to read the Bible. Remember that God is greater than Satan, and begin your fight by asking God to help you to find a regular *time* and *place* to have your daily devotions. Then decide on a *plan* for reading the Bible and praying.[2]

---

1. John Piper, "How to Pray for the Pastoral Staff," Desiring God, March 16, 2005, http://www.desiringgod.org/resource-library/taste-see-articles/how-to-pray-for-the-pastoral-staff.

2. One helpful children's Bible-reading plan is found in the back of the ESV Children's Bible, published by Crossway.

The suggestions below might be helpful in establishing a life-giving Bible devotional time.

- Begin with *prayer.* Ask God to open your mind and your heart.
- *Read* the passage carefully one or more times.
- Use a journal and/or *write* in your Bible. Mark meaningful verses and write about your observations, questions, conclusions, and prayers. What is God asking you to think, be, and do? Here is another thought from Pastor John Piper:

> Writing is a way of seeing that is deeper and sharper than most other ways. We see more when we write than when we just read.
>
> I know not how the light is shed,
> Nor understand this lens.
> I only know that there are eyes
> In pencils and in pens.[3]

- *Worship* God for who He is, *confess* sin, *thank* God for His daily mercies, *ask* God for your needs. Ask God to help you be a doer of His Word.

3.John Piper, "If My Words Abide in You . . ." Desiring God, January 3, 1993, http://www.desiringgod.org/resource-library/sermons/if-my-words-abide-in-you.

children desiring God

This storybook was adapted from *I Stand in Awe*, a lower-elementary midweek Bible curriculum published by Children Desiring God (CDG). If you would like to further explore biblical studies with your child, resources are available from Children Desiring God.

Children Desiring God is a nonprofit ministry that Sally Michael and her husband, David Michael, helped to establish in the late 1990s. CDG publishes God-centered, Bible-saturated, Christ-exalting resources to help parents and churches train their children spiritually in the hope that the next generation will see and embrace Jesus Christ as the one who saves and satisfies the soul. Resources include curricula for children of nursery age through youth (see sequence chart on following page), parenting booklets, and Bible memory resources. Free parenting and Christian education training audio and video resources are also available online.

Please contact us if we can partner with you for the joy of the next generation.

childrendesiringGOD.org
info@childrendesiringGOD.org

SUNDAY SCHOOL	
Nursery	**A Sure Foundation** A Philosophy and Curriculum for Ministry to Infants and Toddlers
Preschool	**He Established a Testimony** Old Testament Stories for Young Children
Preschool	**He Has Spoken By His Son** New Testament Stories for Young Children

	SUNDAY SCHOOL	MIDWEEK
K	**Jesus, What a Savior!** A Study for Children on Redemption	**He Has Been Clearly Seen** A Study for Children on Seeing and Delighting in God's Glory
1	**The ABCs of God** A Study for Children on the Greatness and Worth of God	**I Stand in Awe** A Study for Children on the Bible
2	**Faithful to All His Promises** A Study for Children on the Promises of God	(Children Desiring God will announce plans for this title in the future.)
3	**In the Beginning . . . Jesus** A Chronological Study for Children on Redemptive History	**The Way of the Wise** A Study for Children on Wisdom and Foolishness
4	**To Be Like Jesus** A Study for Children on Following Jesus	**I Will Build My Church** A Study for Children on the Church (future release)
5	**How Majestic Is Your Name** A Study for Children on the Names and Character of God	**Fight the Good Fight** A Study for Children on Persevering in Faith
6	**My Purpose Will Stand** A Study for Children on the Providence of God	**Pour Out Your Heart Before Him** A Study for Children on Prayer and Praise in the Psalms (future release)
7	**Your Word Is Truth** A Study for Youth on Seeing All of Life through the Truth of Scripture	**Abiding in Jesus** A Study for Youth on Trusting Jesus and Encouraging Others
8	**Teach Me Your Way** A Study for Youth on Surrender to Jesus and Submission to His Way	**Rejoicing in God's Good Design** A Study for Youth on Biblical Manhood and Womanhood

Also by Sally Michael

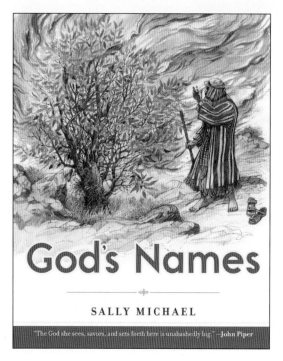

When you want to get to know someone, where do you start? How do you introduce yourself?

Usually you start with someone's name.

God knows this—and he doesn't have just one name to share with us, either! The Bible gives us many names for God and tells us what they all mean. And when we learn a new name for God, we learn something new about him, too!

This book is for you and your children to read together. Every chapter teaches something new and helps put you—and your children—on the right track in your relationship with God.

God has left his names with his people so they can know him . . . and through these pages your children can know him too.

"The God she sees, savors, and sets forth here is unabashedly big. Not distant and uncaring. But great enough to make his caring count."
    —JOHN PIPER, Pastor for Preaching and Vision, Bethlehem Baptist Church, Minneapolis, MN

"Sally Michael creatively helps parents to lead their children through a fun and fascinating exploration of the various ways God's names reveal the beauty and power of his character and actions."
    —JUSTIN TAYLOR, Managing Editor, *ESV Study Bible*

"Grandparents and parents and all the extended family, as well as those who make up the church of the living God—all have a divine unction to pass along God's truth to the hearts of our children! Sally Michael has given us an excellent tool in *God's Names* to do just that!"
    —DOROTHY PATTERSON, General Editor of *The Woman's Study Bible* and Professor of Theology in Woman's Studies, Southwestern Baptist Theological Seminary

Also by Sally Michael

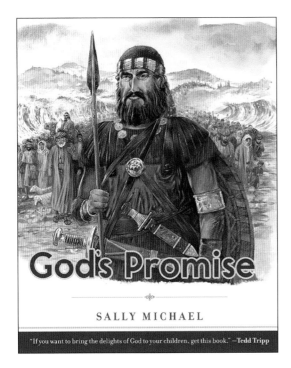

This book, for you and your children to read together, will help them learn these promises and put their own confidence in them. Each chapter looks at a new promise and explores it in the context of a Bible story.

God has left his promises with his people so they can trust him . . . and through these pages your children can trust him too.

"This engaging, attractively illustrated book teaches not only the promises of the Bible, but also the character of the God who makes and keeps his promises."
—TEDD TRIPP, President of Shepherding the Heart Ministries

You have probably seen your children's eyes light up at receiving a present.

How excited would they be to get a present directly from God?

God already has a present to offer your children. And you can be the one who helps them discover it.

God has left all of his children many promises through his Word as gifts that flow from his goodness and love. Each one is backed up by his power and trustworthy character, so we can be confident in them.

"This book is clear, profound, helpful, and at every point grounded with faith and confidence in who God is. A tremendous resource!"
—ELIZABETH GROVES, Lecturer in Old Testament, Westminster Seminary

"Sally Michael does not sugarcoat any of the more difficult promises, but explains them in a way that shows a high view of God. . . . I highly recommend it."
—MARTHA PEACE, Biblical Counselor, Co-author of *The Faithful Parent*

Also by Sally Michael

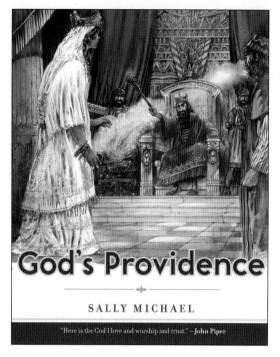

All parents want their children to feel secure.

How reassuring would it be for your child to know that nothing is outside God's control?

Every person, every circumstance, and every action is part of God's plan—a plan that works all things for the good of those who love him. This is God's providence, a doctrine that brings us joy even as it staggers our understanding.

Can a child grasp this important, encouraging truth?

Sally Michael believes that a child who can embrace God's providence can rest in God's sovereign care, and she uses simple truths to help you explain God's providence to all your children. She moves on to show children how God's providence applies to all of life and creation . . . including themselves.

How many fears, worries, frustrations, and tears would be spared if your children truly understood and rested in the providence of God?

"My heart soars with worship and joy and zeal as I page through Sally's new book, *God's Providence*. . . . Here is a foundation for life that is solid enough to sustain parents and children through the hardest times they will ever face. . . . And here is practical application for children and those who love them enough to teach them."
—JOHN PIPER, Author; Associate Pastor for Preaching and Vision, Chancellor, Bethlehem College and Seminary

"Sally Michael has written a primer on God's providence that is richly biblical and theological. This is a helpful resource for parents to introduce their children to God's constant watching and working in our world, and one that provides numerous opportunities for reflection and discussion."
—BRANDON D. CROWE, Associate Professor of New Testament, Westminster Theological Seminary

Also by Sally Michael

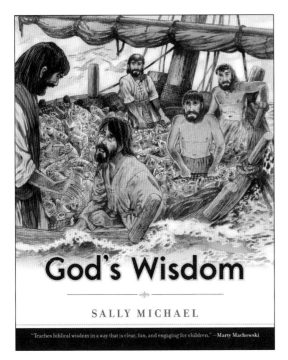

God's Wisdom

SALLY MICHAEL

"Teaches biblical wisdom in a way that is clear, fun, and engaging for children." —Marty Machowski

Every day our children are confronted with the call of wisdom and the call of foolishness.

Which call will they answer?

All of us, down to the youngest child, are born on the path of foolishness. Only God can incline your child's heart toward the path of wisdom—and he can use your example and diligent instruction to do it.

Through these teachings and stories from the Bible, Sally Michael describes for parents and children the characteristics of the foolish and the wise, contrasts for them the way of wisdom with the way of foolishness, and shows them the end result of each path.

Explore these two paths with your own child, and let the words of Proverbs encourage them on the life-giving path of wisdom.

"Sally Michael seamlessly weaves New Testament and Old Testament stories together to teach biblical wisdom in a way that is clear, fun, and engaging for children. Her compelling word pictures and analogies make difficult concepts easier to grasp."
—MARTY MACHOWSKI, Pastor, Author of *Long Story Short* and *The Gospel Story Bible*

"This book is filled with essential biblical wisdom, conveyed in a manner that is wonderfully accessible to children. Additionally, it gives parents numerous practical ideas for applying God's wisdom to the heart and to every area of life."
—JILL NELSON, Curriculum Author, *Children Desiring God*

"Once again, Sally Michael has used her fervent love for Christ and her keen understanding of the Scriptures to help parents and children. . . . I'm very excited to put this book into the hands of parents."
—DEEPAK REJU, Associate Pastor, Capitol Hill Baptist Church, Washington, D.C.

Also by Sally Michael

Sally Michael provides the framework for parents to train their children in the fight of faith. In this full-color, illustrated "battle plan," she uses the gospel message to introduce children to the state of their hearts, then awakens them to the many battlegrounds that surround us—both in our own sinful hearts and from the enemy's attacks.

She then encourages children to be fighters, giving them a biblical battle strategy to depend on God, resist the enemy, and stand strong!

Parents work hard to protect their children from danger.

But are we helping to guard them in the spiritual battle that already rages around them?

Whether he consciously takes sides or not, every person is in the middle of spiritual warfare. None of us can choose to sit on the sidelines—and even our children are not exempt!

So rather than trying to shield them from the very real war around them, why not equip them, as early as possible, to take an active role and fight back?

"The Christian life is no Disney adventure. It's a dangerous journey to the Celestial City, and we spend much of it fighting for faith and for *the* faith. Our children need to learn early on what the battle is all about, what it's like to fight, and how to survive."

—JON BLOOM, President, Desiring God

"*God's Battle* is a theologically rich resource for parents and pastors who want to give children a God-sized vision to fight the good fight of the faith. I highly recommend it."

—JOSH MULVIHILL, Pastor to Children and Families, Grace Church, Eden Prairie, Minnesota